*Public sector*

managerial effectiveness

Public sector
managerial effectiveness
Theory and practice
in the National Health Service

Hugh Flanagan and
Peter Spurgeon

Open University Press
Buckingham · Philadelphia

Open University Press
Celtic Court
22 Ballmoor
Buckingham
MK18 1XW

and
1900 Frost Road, Suite 101
Bristol, PA 19007, USA

First Published 1996

A catalogue record of this book is available from the British Library

ISBN 0–335–15776–9 (pbk)   0–335–15777–7 (hbk)

Library of Congress Cataloging-in-Publication Data
Flanagan, Hugh. 1948–
    Public sector managerial effectiveness : theory and practice in the NHS / Hugh Flanagan and Peter Spurgeon.
        p.   cm.
    Includes bibliographical references (p.   ) and index.
    ISBN 0–335–15777–7(hb). —— ISBN 0–335–15776–9 (pb)
    1. National Health Service (Great Britain)—Administration.
2. Organizational effectiveness.   I. Spurgeon, P. (Peter)
II. Title.
RA412.5.G7F56   1995
362.1'0941—dc20   95–15674
                                                                              CIP

Typeset by Graphicraft Typesetters Ltd, Hong Kong
Printed in Great Britain by St Edmundsbury Press Ltd
Bury St Edmunds, Suffolk

Contents

# *Acknowledgements*

We would like to thank all the colleagues who participated in the data gathering and those who in subsequent discussions have contributed to our ideas.

| Chapter | **Individual and** |
| one | **organisational performance:** |

Individual and organisational performance: a public and private perspective

The context of change for virtually all organisations has become increasingly international, with political instability producing dramatic economic repercussions. Technology and speed of travel has tended to create sequences of economic problems experienced by one country after another. Many countries have had to deal with threats of unemployment, recession and sudden movements in markets. To this extent, all organisations must attempt to tackle the consequences of this turbulence. They are in fact engaged in a process of transition – from operating in a relatively stable environment to one that is much more dynamic.

The characteristics of organisations operating in these contrasting environments are quite different. In a stable environment organisations are typically structured in hierarchical fashion with control exercised at the highest level and problems consequently referred upwards for solution. Management functions largely by precedent and rule with limited responsibility and autonomy at grass roots level. Decisions generally occur via a series of small incremental steps and the focus is internal rather than external. In contrast, the dynamic environment promotes a much greater concern for looking outwards. Everything feels much more unpredictable; there is more competition and the customer is a central force. As a result, organisations need flatter structures and more flexible cross-functional working so that decisions can be made quickly without reference to set rules which have lost their relevance.

Organisations in transition are in pursuit of survival; of course in the current climate many are failing. By definition it is almost as if survival is success. But there are two interlocking concepts embedded in this discussion. The first seeks to understand organisational success or performance while the second at the same time recognises that it is the behaviour of individuals, their effectiveness, that largely determines these outcomes. It is worth remembering that for management educators and trainers the belief that their activities improve managerial behaviour and organisational performance is not only their *raison d'être* but also a source of considerable scepticism to others. The argument developed in this book is that individual managerial effectiveness is a much misused and misunderstood concept. Rather naïvely it tends to be assumed that we all know what constitutes effective managerial behaviour and that it is merely a matter of training staff to perform appropriately. The reality is more complex and much more difficult. Effective management will vary across different organisations. Directly and deliberately, or more likely indirectly and in an unplanned fashion, organisations will set up their own expectations about what is required. Moreover, these behaviours may well change over time as the external circumstances in which organisations operate alter.

Effective management behaviour is therefore contextual. It is contingent upon the situation in which it occurs. This concept will be explored fully in later chapters, but in this first chapter we examine some of the factors that create these contextual influences. The key first source must be the organisation itself and, in particular, what we understand by successful organisations. Also with our focus upon public sector organisations, it is important to be aware of the potential impact of a public or private sector setting upon what is regarded as appropriate behaviour for managers.

The successful organisation

The current vogue to describe success rather simplistically in terms of the 'bottom line' focuses exclusively upon profitability and financial indicators. A wider definition would incorporate aspects such as the stability of the workforce, opportunities for growth, regard for the environment and involvement with the local community. Yet another concept is to ask what does a successful organisation look like, what does it feel like to work in one, and how would you recognise a successful organisation. This particular approach, referred to as 'theories of excellence' or the search for 'universals', was popularised in the 1980s by Peters and Waterman (1982) *In Search of Excellence*, Goldsmith and Clutterbuck (1984) *The Winning Streak* and Harvey-Jones (1988) *Making it Happen*.

The characteristics described by these authors are well known and will not be recounted here. There is, though, remarkable consistency in the factors identified. Successful organisations will tend to exhibit:

- a strong sense of market or customer orientation
- a strong sense of control over the areas that matter but also encouragement of freedom and autonomy
- fairness and responsibility in the way staff are treated
- a clear vision and direction through strong leadership
- simple, clear, responsive structures.

Interestingly, though, this harmony of view is not entirely reinforced by Ouchi's theory 'Z' (1981) explaining the success of Japanese companies. He lists factors such as:

- lifetime employment
- slow evaluation and promotion
- non-specialised career paths
- consensus decision making
- collective responsibility
- holistic concern for employees.

The strong sense of entrepreneurship seems to be missing from this list and as such is confusing, although presumably explained by cultural differences. It should be noted that some of these concepts are being questioned within Japan.

Handy (1989) may offer some integrative concepts to organise these disparate views. Whilst endorsing many of the excellent characteristics, he also suggests that intelligent individuals can only be governed by consent and not by command, that obedience cannot be demanded and that a collegiate culture of colleagues and a shared understanding is the only way to make things happen. As regards success and effectiveness, Handy agrees with the formula $I^3 = AV$, where I stands for intelligence, information and ideas and AV means added value in cash or in kind. In a competitive society, brains on their own are not enough; they need good information to work with and ideas to build on if they are going to make value out of knowledge.

This model helpfully serves to reinforce the role of the individual and their intelligence as a contributing force to organisational success. However, most of these ideas are derived from the private sector. The fact that many of the concepts are based upon various versions of profitability explains why there may be limited applicability to the public sector. It may of course also contribute to the rather stereotypic view that the public sector is inefficient and wasteful. However, Sikorski (1993), in reviewing work on the public sector, challenges this perception and demonstrates considerable confusion. He cites evidence from researchers describing the public sector as:

- producing both higher quality and lower quality
- managers having longer tenure and brief tenure for top management
- managers are more risk averse and managers are less risk averse
- taking a long-term view and taking a short-term view.

Relatively little empirical evidence exists that would enable one to clarify whether private or public sector operations are more effective. Dunsire *et al.* (1994) undertook a detailed investigation of a number of large organisations (e.g. British Telecom, Royal Ordnance Factories) who had experienced a change in status. Two of the principal notions explored were that in a move towards private status for all organisations (a) the degree of competition encountered increases; and (b) internal management focus shifts from an input, command-orientated structure to a results orientation. The measures used to assess performance were:

1 productivity
2 change in employment levels
3 financial ratios (profitability).

Their conclusions are largely comforting to our current hypothesis and endeavours in preparing this text. The results are rather contradictory. They report that life is rather more complicated than prescriptive theories might assume. The simple assertion that change in ownership necessarily changes enterprise performance is not supported. Sometimes it does, sometimes it doesn't. The study itself is complex and the authors admit that further study, especially longitudinal, is required; but it illustrates well the difficulty in being overly prescriptive about best practice.

The situation is far from clear. There are dangers in transferring concepts from the private to public sector without some caution. This is particularly important here since we are principally concerned with the public sector and managerial effectiveness within it. Much of the thinking and research concerning an individual's performance involves ideas from the private sector currently being transposed to a public sector context.

The public sector context

There has been a remarkable period of change in the public sector, so much so that the term 'new public sector' has been coined to indicate the radical nature of these changes. It has been suggested that the Conservative British government of 1979 entered power with a clearly formulated plan for public sector reform. However, close analysis of legislation through the period (as yet continuous) of Conservative government in Britain suggests that it was rather more piecemeal and reactive than one might imagine. None the less it is true that the liberal economics extolled by Thatcher and the merits of a profit-seeking competitive economic system have found consistent embodiment in the public choice theory.

The most significant changes in the public sector may be summarised as privatisation, managerialism and a process of enabling new approaches to the provision of services. Privatisation is probably the simplest concept, involving the transfer of ownership of organisations from public to private sector bodies. Various components of the public sector have been subject to this process in various guises – deregulation of bus services, contracting out specific local government functions such as leisure provision, the concept of 'opting out' in education and housing and the emergence of trust hospitals in the NHS. Despite much workforce opposition, the policy would seem to be well received by the voters, judging by their continuing support. The public sector has been dramatically changed by this process, with over 50 per cent of the public sector transferred into private delivery agencies (Marsh 1991).

Managerialism has also found expression within the public sector. Initially efforts were focused upon reducing expenditure and the promotion of cost-consciousness. Policy makers recognised that in order to sustain gains from such initiatives it was important for the public sector to acquire an alternative managerial culture. The process involved three key elements:

- A 'business-like' approach where management practices based upon a private sector ethos were to replace a more traditional professional-based value system. The latter was felt to favour the professional providers over the user.
- A more responsive decision-making process where the consensus based decisions, typical of the Public Sector, by which interest groups delayed progress, would be replaced.
- A tougher, 'make it happen' approach so that managers at various levels would have the power to decide and implement.

(Isaac Henry and Palmer 1991: 11)

At the same time budgets were decentralised so that large bureaucracies were broken down and replaced by smaller accountable units. Further private sector concepts such as consumerism and market forces have become common parlance in the public sector. Of course, as clients become customers they require choice, which has important repercussions since it requires that alternative forms of provision come into existence.

It is this process that has led to the enabling role of the public sector. 'Enabling' is at the same time an individual procedure supporting and empowering people to influence the nature and quality of services, as well as differentiating the function of public sector organisations by allowing them to be purchasers and/or providers of services. Organisations have adopted different stances upon this issue. Some local authorities have withdrawn largely from the provision of services, seeing their role as strategically helping the community to access the best, most cost-effective services, wherever they come from. The outcome overall is a greater diversity in the range and function of public service organisations.

There can be little doubt, though, that the concept of performance management has become a core concept in the public sector, indeed some would say, the big idea of the 1990s. It is a term that captures many of the private sector practices that have been advocated for inclusion in the public sector. Performance management, or value for money as it is often called, is concerned with the relationship between input (resources) and the use of these resources as efficiently as possible, and the outputs, or what is achieved through the use of these resources. For this reason, performance management is often described as being concerned with:

- economy (the resources used to produce a service or product)
- efficiency (maximising the use of these resources in producing the service)
- effectiveness (the outcome or impact of the product upon the client).

(Isaac-Henry *et al.* 1993: 39)

Some authors, particularly those more concerned with public sector activities, would also add the concept of equity, defined as justice or fairness in the use and distribution of resources (Bovaird *et al.* 1988).

Any form of performance management must involve the monitoring and assessment of objectives set. In the private sector there tends to be a range of financially orientated measures missing in the public sector. As a consequence, a number of process or surrogate measures are invented such as school examination league tables, waiting time for patients seeking health treatment, or number of users of a particular service. The demand for performance indicators in the public sector is, in part, central government seeking to retain and control the system it is notionally trying to set free. In creating such measures there has often been a failure to ensure true internal ownership of the measure so that staff within the organisation understand and accept their capacity to influence the outcome. Mostly in public sector contexts outcomes are determined by factors outside the control of those working within the provider organisation.

Similarly there has been a rather naïve assumption that precise measures of outcome and output exist by which good and bad performance can be readily assessed. Rarely is this the case. Carter (1989) has a very nice phrase for such measures, describing them as 'tin-openers', the implication being that they tend to open a 'can of worms'. This highlights the critically interactive nature of different parts of a service and the relative lack of control that can be exerted.

Of particular interest here is the point that such performance indicators have considerable managerial implication. The prescriptive indicator is a top–down management tool. Government policy via performance targets epitomises a command style of management, while their rhetoric talks of greater local autonomy. This is a complex dilemma for those in government who, whilst advocating greater local autonomy, cannot accept the loss of their own central power.

Performance indicators may be helpful in some cases, but they need to be treated with caution because they can focus upon sub-elements of a service and sometimes divert resources, inappropriately, to this particular aspect. Clearly one of the issues emerging is that successful performance management practices must take into account the culture and context of the organisation into which they are introduced.

There are those who have expressed strong misgivings as to the appropriateness of transferring concepts from the private to public sector. Stewart (1989b) writes:

> The real danger is that the unthinking adoption of the Private Sector model prevents the development of an approach to management in the Public Services in general or to the social services in particular based on their distinctive purposes, conditions and tasks.
>
> (p. 48)

He argues that management is not the same in all situations and therefore takes a form contingent upon the context. Marketing, for example, is a classic private sector concern that has an individual focus and is concerned with demand, generating it and meeting it. This is not the case with the public sector, where demand is generally beyond the supply. The criteria for limit upon supply are usually set by political forces. Stewart's thesis is essentially that neither private nor public management styles are better than each other: they are different and distinctive.

The argument is taken further by Harrow and Willcocks (1990). Their argument is based around uncertainties in the nature of managerial behaviour. None the less the thrust of their position is similar to that of Stewart. They offer, in summary:

> there emerges no coherent, systematic, agreed view of management or what managers do, or what they should be doing in private sector organisation. It is ironic, therefore, that in a period when the nature of management has been questioned as never before, the UK Public Services have found themselves judged against 'traditional' management criteria, which are themselves judged suspect and have been found wanting.
>
> (p. 285)

It is not appropriate here to explore in detail the differences between operating in the public or private domain. The discussion by Harrow and Willcocks is an excellent review of these issues. The conclusion from their analysis is important, though, in terms of this text, for they suggest that the differences will have implications for managerial behaviour. Thus our concern must be to understand how these forces act upon managers to establish varying conceptions of effectiveness.

Management and effectiveness

The many studies of managerial activities have failed to produce a clear picture of effective management (Hales 1986). Hales suggests that, in part, this can be attributed to the range of samples and contexts examined, but perhaps more importantly it is due to the lack of any coherent explanatory concepts which can be applied to all managerial behaviour. Hales argues that role theory would offer such an overall framework as it sits between the individual personality and organisation influences.

Fonda and Stewart (1994) develop this argument further by suggesting the particular merits of a role-based analysis are that it is inherently interpersonal and hence focuses upon the interactions between individuals, which is a vital component of managerial behaviour. Moreover the concentration upon interaction highlights the powerful determining force played by expectations in shaping behaviour (Sayles 1979). It is the expectations held by an individual's role set that elicit particular behaviours. A manager therefore behaves in accord with the expectations of those with whom he/she interacts. Of course it is possible for the manager to exert pressure and hence influence expectations of his/her own behaviour. This may well represent very skilful managerial behaviour, in such a way that the manager brings about an alignment between the expectations of others and his/her own capacity to fulfil these expectations. Fonda and Stewart (1994: 88) speak of this as expectation enactment – the carrying out of expectations of others. A vital comment from their work for our study of individual effectiveness centres upon the view that 'A manager could also enact expectations by trying to define the criteria used to evaluate job performance or by sending messages or influence attempts regarding expectations others should or might hold'. Thus the judgement of effectiveness becomes a highly dynamic process with two or more sources exchanging pressures and forces, often in an unstated manner, about how such a judgement is to be made. This of course offers a valuable conceptual explanation but at the same time illustrates the complexity involved in studying this apparently subjective, flexible and moving relationship. More successful managers are likely to be effective in influencing the expectations held by others, especially in the area of performance management, and hence are more likely to be judged effective. Clearly one of the strands we will examine later in this book is how this negotiated set of expectations plays a vital role in the assessment of individual performance and effectiveness.

This conception of effectiveness is fundamental to our approach and is supported by Willcocks (1992), who suggests 'that effectiveness is subjective and socially constructed, it is not (much as many would like it to be and indeed insist upon treating as such) an external observable fact' (p. 6). Not only will the expectations of the work group influence our perception of effectiveness, but so too will political forces within an organisation. These political forces will in turn shape individual expectations, and so on. Clearly there is an interaction. We might think of the political dynamics of an organisation as its context and culture. Thus we move to our principal thesis that individual effectiveness is a contextually based phenomenon, and hence we need to understand the pervading culture of an organisation in order to understand how managerial performance will be assessed.

These issues are most effectively captured by the writing of Moss Kanter and Summers (1987) and Meek (1988). The former identifies very clearly the great complexity in assessing performance in not-for-profit organisations, and raises issues such as whether measurement should focus upon individual goals or societal goals – at organisational or sub-unit level – and the general multidimensionality of those with a stake in influencing organisational goals. The complexity of organisational goals is of course then reflected in a lack of clarity in the way individuals working within the organisation feel they ought to behave.

Rather simplistically these expectations, their creation and dissemination have become labelled organisational culture. Meek rather scathingly criticises this approach as implying that organisational culture is something to be manipulated and produced. She argues 'that culture should be regarded as something that an organisation "is", not as something that an organisation "has": it is not an independent variable, nor can it be created, discovered or destroyed by the whims of management' (Meek 1988: 274). This is (or should be) perhaps a rather sobering thought for the many management consultants and their clients setting out to create a new organisational culture. Does this mean that organisational culture is unimportant? On the contrary, what her argument is saying is that 'culture' as a term has use in relation to the interpretation of observed concrete behaviour. Thus for our purpose of understanding individual managerial effectiveness, this important point focuses upon the identification of behaviours individuals may believe to be appropriate and the search to understand how these may be related to symbols that represent and suggest the culture of the organisation within which they are working.

Structure of the book

In the next chapter (Chapter 2) we explore the subjective nature of the concept of managerial effectiveness and the importance of sharing different perceptions. We attempt to define managerial effectiveness and illustrate how dependent concepts of appropriateness are upon elements of the situation. This theme is further developed in Chapters 3 and 4, where we examine how managerial effectiveness has been used in practice in a range of organisational contexts, and the thinking processes and mental models involved in how managers develop their own personal models of managerial effectiveness.

Chapter 5 explores the organisational and cultural factors that influence perspectives of effectiveness. It also touches upon the role of the human resource function as a crucial agent in this link between expected behaviour and performance. Appraisal is perhaps the key process here, and this is discussed in detail in Chapter 6.

Chapter 7 describes a study undertaken by the authors which illustrates the variability in practice in the way effectiveness is understood, and demonstrates the differences between individuals and organisations. Finally Chapter 8 attempts to provide some guidance to those who have to make judgements of others about effectiveness as to how the process can be approached and improved now and in the near future context of the public sector.

The critical link between individual effectiveness and organisational success

If any public sector organisation is to be effective in terms of meeting the expectation set by national goals and policy guidelines, then its collective effect on individual manager behaviour must support the achievement of those goals. However, as we have made explicit in the previous chapter, the model of effectiveness adopted here is a contingent rather than systems model. The key implications of this assumption are:

1 that effectiveness is a subjective rather than absolute concept, and
2 that this subjective vision of effective behaviour is defined and determined by factors within each organisation.

In order that an organisation achieves its overall goal it is therefore critical that it is clear about its process for sharing expectations about managerial behaviour. This process both enables managers to direct their behaviour to appropriate goals and helps the organisation to support, encourage and develop behaviours consistent with achieving success.

A manager's view or perception of effectiveness is conditioned by his or her experience of working in a particular organisation. Managers consciously or unconsciously recognise organisational signs and symbols and the expectations of others and act accordingly. A successful organisation must therefore understand whether it is giving the 'right' message to its managers. This model needs to be made explicit both collectively and individually. It may be thought of as the creation of behavioural expectations that parallel and complement other organisational constraints such as mission, corporate culture and rules.

A manager's own perceptions of effectiveness will govern their expectation of others. For example, the beliefs held by top managers about effective managerial behaviour will have a major influence on their subordinates and will affect decisions on selection, appraisal and development.

Similarly, a manager's own behaviour will be governed by their perception and beliefs about effectiveness, in particular what they believe they have to do to be deemed effective in the organisation in which they currently work. If a manager reads his or her situation accurately then they are much more likely to perform well, within the expectations of that organisation. But two things can go wrong. The manager may not be able to read the situation accurately, in other words they may not possess the necessary skills and insights; and/ or the organisation may be ambiguous and have difficulty in communicating its message. Either way the result will adversely affect the overall performance of the organisation to a greater or lesser degree, depending on the position and nature of the job the manager undertakes.

In order to avoid the collective effect of poor performance by individual managers, an organisation needs to understand the perceptions or beliefs its managers hold about the nature of managerial effectiveness. Possession of this knowledge allows the organisation to address the concept of 'organisational fit', i.e. whether managers' beliefs and behaviours are consistent with those desired and how modification of them (if necessary) may be achieved.

Interestingly, many recent approaches to developing and improving organisations (total quality management/management competencies), whilst apparently more systems-orientated, in part incorporate some key elements of a more contingent approach. Such approaches emphasise specific skills or competencies required by managers (competency approach) or the development of a quality-orientated culture that defines the behaviours needed to improve the service provided. Although the overriding objective of such models is enhanced organisational performance, they incorporate the notion of making more explicit the behaviours required to achieve identified goals. Thus in accord with the contingency organisationally specific approach they offer greater clarity and definition of the behaviour sought from individual managers.

The managerial effectiveness approach discussed in this book is in a number of ways an organisation-specific competency approach. The authors would argue that for any one organisation there is merit in reinventing the wheel in terms of identifying the particular skills and behaviours that are perceived by managers to represent effective management in that organisation at that time. It is the process of managers articulating, sharing and understanding the individual and collective picture of effectiveness that is important, as it allows the organisation to examine the value of such perceptions to the fulfilment of its purpose and the achievement of its business goals. Borrowing sets of words or competencies from another organisation, even a common set derived from a range of organisations, is only useful if they are debated in terms of meaning and value to the organisation in question, and then internalised and operationalised by its managers. The culture of organisations differs, sometimes markedly, sometimes subtly; what works in one may not work in another. There needs to be a thorough understanding of the influences in the organisation which produce the individual and collective perceptions of effective management.

Subjective perceptions of effective management

The concept of managerial effectiveness is an inherently complex subject often treated with cavalier simplicity and unexamined convictions and assumptions. There is a multitude of cultural influences with performance implications for organisations, affecting a range of managerial processes and systems including selection, judgement and decision making about key people, appraisal and the training and development of managers. These individual decisions have a cumulative effect on the organisation's ability to be effective or even to define clearly what it is there to do.

An example from a public sector workshop on individual performance review conducted by one of the authors may help illustrate how individual expectations affect the operation and outcome of performance review or appraisal systems, and ultimately the performance of the organisation as a whole. A subordinate manager was described as showing more 'leadership' than a colleague at a similar level of authority undertaking a similar role in the organisation. A prolonged discussion, which tried to pin down exactly what this person did that demonstrated 'leadership', eventually focused on the fact that they spent a lot of their own time in the evenings and at weekends organising and running social events which were perceived to do a lot for staff morale and the *esprit de corps* of the organisation. Needless to say this particular activity had never been identified within the formalities of the performance review system. Even after it had been identified it was felt inappropriate to include it formally as it could not be seen as a part of the official job of the individuals concerned. In addition, the significance for organisational performance was not clear. Further discussion of this issue between senior managers did not lead to any resolution as there were clearly differing sets of expectations held of subordinates and different views about making such unofficial expectations explicit. Some felt it quite appropriate to have this type of expectation or requirement even if it were not made explicit because it illustrated the degree to which motivation, leadership or any other facet of effective management could be freely demonstrated by an individual of their own volition. In other words, in this particular organisation in the public sector, managers were expected to put more time and energy into their job than the official contract required or than was described in any of the existing systems designed to clarify, for the manager, what was expected of him or her. Whilst at the same time it was not really clear how this attribute of individual effectiveness related to improved organisational performance.

This is one particular example from one particular organisation with its own culture and management style. In this case it could be said that if a manager guessed or sensed correctly what was expected of him or her they would be seen as more effective than their colleagues, but whether it would ultimately lead to a higher performance rating would depend largely on which senior manager undertook the performance review. Even more importantly, the connection between this implicit expectation and ultimate organisational performance was not clear. It seems that when a manager is described as effective or successful or good, the inspiration for the use of the term can have many different origins. It may be something to do with the manager's personality, his or her relationship with seniors and peers, major tasks or objectives completed or, as illustrated above, something extra that a particular manager puts into a job. It is not unusual to find that an opinion seems to have been formed on the basis of very limited contact with the individual concerned, or that the opinion is based on one particular facet of the individual's behaviour dress, experience, education, etc. – a typical halo/horns effect bearing no known or clear link to organisational performance and outcomes.

Changing organisational contexts and circumstances may dictate whether a particular manager is viewed as successful or not at any point in time. For example, if as a result of organisational change a manager is made accountable to a different person who has a different perception of effectiveness, not only will the new boss quickly develop a different view of their subordinate's effectiveness, different expectations derived from different perceptions may begin to condition the subordinate to behave differently. This assumes of course that the subordinate is both sensitive to these different expectations and is capable of adapting to meet them.

The manager who is deemed to be effective, or ineffective, in one organisation may be judged quite differently in another organisation. For example, when a senior manager in a public sector organisation is not appointed to 'their' job but is successful in obtaining a post of similar seniority and role in another public sector organisation where he or she is deemed to be effective. Similarly, an apparently successful manager from the private sector may be unable to make an effective transition to a management post in a public sector organisation. A classic and somewhat topical example of this type of situational specificity is the relationship between a chief executive of an NHS trust and his/her chairperson. This can be a personal style mismatch; equally it may well be an increasingly explicit awareness that the two individuals do not agree about the behaviours and actions required to deliver organisational success. It is for this reason that great emphasis is given to this vital relationship in the establishment of trust boards.

Like truth and beauty we can progressively refine our own view or definition of effectiveness but to reach agreement with others we have to locate the concepts in a specific context. It will also be necessary to try to reach agreement with others on the meaning of words and phrases used in attempting to define effectiveness.

Leadership as a factor in managerial effectiveness

A similar situation may be observed by use of the term 'leadership' to describe an aspect of effective managerial behaviour. In a recent research study (Flanagan 1990) into managerial effectiveness carried out in the NHS, during detailed interviews among 19 senior general managers, five of them directly used the term 'leadership' in their description of effective managerial behaviour, e.g. 'he is a good leader' or 'has good leadership skills'. In order to understand their use of the term and the meaning ascribed to these phrases they were asked to explain them in more detail. This produced at least nine further descriptions, which are set out in Chapter 7. They suggest quite different approaches to the behaviours and beliefs managers associate with 'leadership', which is one aspect of effective management.

In recent years the idea of 'leadership' appears to have taken over from that of 'management', especially in relation to more senior 'managerial' posts. Leaders seem to be seen as different from managers, just as in the past managers were often distinguished from administrators within the public sector. Recent studies of leadership distinguish the terms by describing leadership as having more of an emotional content based on a clear vision which, when clearly and enthusiastically communicated to other people, excites and motivates them to adopt and pursue that vision, whilst management is more about organising things so that the vision can be accomplished and incorporates planning, strategy, objectives, settings, etc. In the past the stance taken in the public sector was that management was something that was mainly done in the private sector, whereas 'administration', which might be defined as the carrying out of policies and being publicly accountable for doing so (Stewart 1989a), was the province of the public sector. Administration was an activity based on the notion that publicly accountable servants of the State were there to make sure that policies were implemented and be seen to be implemented, which produced a requirement for documentation in order to provide evidence of decisions that were taken and how they were in practice. The term 'officer' or 'administrator', used mainly in the public sector in the past, has largely been dropped and the term 'manager' or 'director' is now largely used for posts in the public sector, indicating the different roles they have to play. The difference between a manager and a leader is the difference between one who directs and one who points the way. The leader's role is to identify and symbolise what is important.

It would seem that leadership is an essential requirement within most managers' jobs since pointing out what is important is akin to identifying the purpose of a job or the organisation.

Performance management systems

As the previous chapter has made clear, during the last ten years or so public sector organisations have increasingly been subject to formal systems and processes based on identifying specific objectives and targets for achievement with performance, both individual and organisational, being measured against this. This is also the situation in private sector organisations and has been encompassed in the term 'performance management'. For example, the individual performance review system introduced into the NHS (PM/86/10) is based on evaluating performance in terms of the achievement of agreed objectives (Department of Health and Social Security 1986). In other words, performance management focuses on clarifying what is expected of the manager and then giving feedback on how well they meet these expectations. However, even a superficial discussion with the managers concerned with the objective-setting process quickly moves into descriptions of how they go about achieving objectives in relation to the context in which they work. The focus tends to be on the behaviour managers adopt in coping with their own organisations. Asking managers to explain what they mean by descriptions of effective management such as 'shows leadership' (as discussed above) injects considerable variety into what may start as an apparently shared definition or list of adjectives about effective managerial behaviour. Research has shown (Machin 1981) that any management-by-objectives-based approach such as the one operating in the NHS and in many other public sector organisations, considerably over-simplifies the real complexity of a hierarchical objective-setting process. Machin cites examples of where up to 70 per cent of the expectations held of the manager were lateral or diagonal, in other words, they came from outside the manager–subordinate relationship on which the objective assessment process is purportedly based.

More recent research and practice (IPM 1992) indicates that more organisations are going for multiple appraisals involving other managers, peers and even subordinates and place individually based schemes in a broader context of systems for managing performance. This is discussed more fully in Chapter 6.

The context of many public sector organisations makes it difficult for those involved to provide a definitive answer to the fundamental question of why certain objectives are identified and targeted and, by implication, others ignored. In many public sector organisations clarifying key and long-term objectives proves to be a remarkably difficult exercise given the political and public context in which the management processes are undertaken. Again taking the example of the NHS, there are particular difficulties with clarifying the organisational purpose or outcome for which the NHS exists. For example, is a patient treated successfully in a hospital a sign of the effectiveness of the NHS or its ineffectiveness? This must take us back to the essential question as to the purpose of the NHS and the argument about whether it is there to treat the sick or actually prevent people getting sick (Klein 1982). More recently, is the achievement of a higher throughput of patients, with concomitant increase in community care costs, an acceptable objective goal or not? The inherent conflict and contradictions in public sector organisations reinforce the need for a contingency approach to determining effectiveness.

The meaning of managerial effectiveness

The essential nature of managerial work is 'to do something' or to organise others to do that something, and will depend on the type of job, its location in the organisation, the nature of the organisation, etc. The use of the word 'effective' in relation to what a manager does implies that the 'doing' is fulfilling some expectation or purpose. Therefore to be effective, the manager must 'do' things that are assumed to be necessary and relevant by the organisation in which he or she works. In some cases, the expectations may be explicit and set out in terms of individual objectives or contributions to corporate goals. On the other hand, they may be implied in terms of the cultural norms of behaviour expected of and adopted by managers in a particular organisation. Or they may be both. Even if expectations are apparently explicit in terms of what a manager should do – that is, the objectives which he or she should concentrate on and pursue – there may also be a range of implicit expectations about how he or she should go about achieving the objectives.

'Effectiveness must be supplemented with a statement of purpose, intention or function' (Burgoyne 1976). Any dictionary definition of effectiveness starts in a similar way, e.g. 'effective' – productive of or capable of producing a result, and applying it to the context of management implies that we need to be precise about what we mean by management and its function, related to the needs and purpose of the organisation in which the managers we are concerned with actually work. What are the essential outputs which demonstrate or fulfil the purpose of the organisation to which the manager contributes by his or her work?

We have already identified that the essential outputs of the NHS and other public sectors cannot be easily defined. But if the context in which an NHS manager works is defined in more parochial terms, rather than talking about the NHS as a whole, for example a single hospital or community service, then output can be defined in terms of curing or caring for the sick, the elderly, the handicapped, etc.; various qualitative and quantitative measures can be applied to assess performance, e.g. how many patients were treated, how many survived for what period, etc. An effective manager can be described as someone who creates, operationalises and sustains organisational operations that satisfy as far as possible the diverse values and interests of those affected by the operations. The process of defining such purposes or operations may highlight divergent views not only as to the purpose of individual jobs and the requirements or expectations of the job holder, but also about the nature and purpose of the organisation. The essential problem may be obtaining agreement about the primary purpose, intention or function of the organisation and its key objectives. Discussing the performance or effectiveness of any organisation provokes a debate on how the objectives of that organisation and the criteria for performance assessment are to be defined. What is its purpose? What are the people who manage it expected to do? Without such agreement, selecting the appropriate operations to satisfy 'the diverse values and interests of those affected', in any kind of objective terms, could be an almost impossible exercise. The effect of this would be to make any concept of managerial effectiveness not only totally subjective but also so diverse and inconsistent as to be unsustainable.

'General prescriptions of effectiveness are most unlikely to be a perfect or even a good fit (for a particular organisation). We believe it is much more important to be able to diagnose what the characteristics are of effective management in a given firm, at a given level, and the evidence we have suggests that we are right' (Stewart and Stewart 1981a: 51). Using the repertory grid technique, Valerie and Andrew Stewart identified 60 to 90 characteristics which distinguished the effective from the ineffective manager, with only a third of these consistent across organisations and jobs. The remaining characteristics reflect the uniqueness of particular jobs derived from the type of job or the role undertaken, the type of organisation, history and development, its particular culture and style, whether it was a public or private sector organisation and the general environment in which the job and the organisation were located. They concluded that there was no such thing as the universally effective manager.

Situational sensitivity

The situational or contingent view of effectiveness emphasises the importance of any individual manager being able to recognise the expectations held of him and her by others and then making the right choices about which expectations he or she will attempt to meet. This underlines the critical importance of two things:

1 That the situation and context – that is, the organisation – in which the manager works must be such that the correct and appropriate expectations are created by the combination of managerial systems and processes that operate within the organisation, i.e. business planning, performance review systems, human resource management and development policies, etc.
2 That the manager is helped to develop the capacity to interpret his or her situation accurately so that they understand fully what is expected of them, and is then helped to enhance or develop the skills and capabilities that will allow them to meet those expectations.

If these two points are not taken into account, the view that a manager is 'effective' will be based solely on the extent to which he or she actually or apparently fulfils the subjective and variable frame of reference that others use for thinking about the 'effectiveness'. 'Decisions about effectiveness are bound to be situational and contingent upon the definition and perspectives of those making the judgement' (Machin and Stewart 1981).

It is therefore critical that organisations define what they mean by effective management, which must be based on a clear understanding and articulation of the purpose and goals and the activities, objectives and behaviours that are required of managers in order to achieve them. Managers make choices about what they will spend their time and effort on within their job based on the beliefs about what is considered important by the organisation, which is conveyed to them through the interaction with other managers, particularly senior managers, and their peer group.

> The most important application for the manager who wants to improve his own effectiveness is in helping him to recognise both the scope that exists for personal choice and the choices that he has made, often unconsciously, in his present job. One of the arts of successful management is the recognition and successful exploitation of the key choices that exist in a job.
>
> (Stewart 1976)

The expectations of others in the organisation could be said to provide the menu from which choices are made by an individual manager. Assuming that the manager is able to identify what is expected, which set or combination of expectations will he or she attempt to satisfy? If the right set of choices are made, the manager will be judged to be effective. But the expectations may not necessarily be based on any 'rational' set of views about what needs to be done to fulfil the purpose of the organisation. The effective manager may be one who, being aware of the different kinds of behaviours that are available and that he or she has the capability to adopt, 'then chooses to engage those appropriate to the environment, the management job, the situation and his own preferences' (Morse and Wagner 1978: 24). In other words, the manager, assuming he or she has the skills to do so, reads the situation and decides which of the predominant or most influential expectations he or she could attempt to satisfy in order to earn the accolade of a good 'successful' or 'effective' manager.

> The skills of reading the situation, i.e. of knowing which are the priorities for attention at any particular time and selecting the most appropriate behaviours, are as important as the skills

required for communication with and acting with others in that situation, and that it was precisely these skills which differentiated a successful from an unsuccessful manager.

(Alban-Metcalfe 1983: 4)

This idea is somewhat akin to the concept of a metacompetence whereby it is proposed that successful managers need to acquire a superordinate skill or competence that allows them to decide when more specific behavioural competencies should be brought in to play. This particular view of effectiveness, or the key attributes and abilities which lead to effective managerial behaviour, is particularly pertinent to organisations where a sustained and cohesive consensus on specific organisational priorities on which managers can focus their effort in the medium to long term is more difficult to achieve. This description could apply in particular to many public sector organisations such as the NHS. In such organisations, any view of effectiveness is likely to be highly situational, both within the same job or organisation over time, as well as from job to job and organisation to organisation. Because the situation is constantly changing, the effective manager becomes the one who can continuously identify and adapt to the changing expectations of the situation he or she is in, making the 'right' choices about what he or she should do or not do. In a public sector organisation like the NHS, the plethora of national priorities combined with the variety of different local circumstances gives different weightings to the national priorities as well as producing more local ones. In such a context, the skill of identifying the key expectations (priorities, objectives or behaviours) others have at any particular point in time, and then being able to do something about them, would seem to be fundamental to being, or being perceived to be, an effective manager.

The term 'effective manager' presupposes a clear and agreed description of what managers are supposed to do, matched against evidence of what they actually do. It does not therefore seem possible to maintain any absolute objective standard against which managers' behaviour and activities can be compared. The standard must be a contingent one. 'One such contingent standard with which to compare actual managerial practice might be what others expect or require managers to do. Good or bad practice may then be conceived in terms of the extent to which managers' performance matches others' expectations' (Hales 1986: 108). The key skill for the organisation would therefore seem to be the need to ensure that these individual managerial linkages (actual to expectations) are then transformed appropriately into overall organisational targets.

The matching of what managers do against what managers are expected to do demands some contextual framework in which to place identified behaviours, i.e. are they appropriate to the circumstances of the job, are they effective? But if it can be argued that managerial effectiveness is perceived as a match between actual and expected behaviour, then from the individual manager's point of view it may not matter if there is no clear purpose or objectives for the organisation as a whole. A manager's main concern in terms of organisational survival and advancement may be simply to be perceived as effective, i.e. to have the reputation of being effective based on 'the capacity of a manager to satisfy a number of possible conflicting constituencies in the course of his or her work' (Tsui 1984: 30). This may be much more important to the individual than worrying about whether or not an organisation as a whole is effective, i.e. whether it is achieving its purpose, however that is defined. As already discussed, expectations may be explicitly stated in terms of objectives or may be implied, or both. Objective-setting processes in many organisations appear to be inadequate in setting out the total expectations senior managers have of their subordinates. The key skill that managers must develop is that needed 'to acquire a greater sensitivity to, and capacity to negotiate among the diversity of role demands, formal or informal, loud or inaudible, made on them' (Hales 1987: 33).

The key factor in defining managerial effectiveness in practice seems to be the type of assumptions, views and opinions that any one manager has and uses, consciously or unconsciously, in explicitly or implicitly formulating the expectations they have about subordinates, colleagues, bosses, etc. Discussion of the term 'effective management' in the abstract is more likely to produce idealised and generalised statements. Discussion of a particular manager in terms of why he or she is seen as effective or ineffective will produce more detailed descriptions. But the problem may be that managers perceive other managers to be effective or not in terms of what they see or believe they see them doing. If it fits with their frame of reference, i.e. their picture of what constitutes managerial effectiveness, and it is deemed to be appropriate to the circumstances, then they will be categorised in the mind of the perceiving manager as 'effective'. Ultimately it is other managers in the organisation who make the decision about each other's effectiveness. Where they have authority in the organisation this is translated into decisions about selection, promotion, training, development and appraisal. The quality of such decisions about subordinates will affect the success of the organisation. The quality of the decision will be dependent on a clear and communicated link between the organisation's purpose and the expectations held of managers in terms of what they do and how they do it.

The referral context – environment – of the organisation interacts with the internal to affect expectations. The impact is likely to be more fundamental for top public sector managers where the constant reappraisal of the nature and structure of public sector organisations provides an ambiguous context with few fixed points for finding individual manager effectiveness.

Chapter	**Understanding managerial**
three	**effectiveness**

This chapter looks at how the term 'managerial effectiveness' is used in practice and how it has been defined in other works. It examines the mental processes involved in the way individual managers build up a picture of effectiveness and discusses how this affects their subsequent behaviour.

Defining managerial effectiveness

To understand managerial effectiveness one must first attempt to define it. One of the most useful summaries of the literature up to the end of the 1970s was that produced by Vicky Langford (1979) particularly in relation to the different meanings ascribed to the term 'managerial effectiveness'. The literature on managerial effectiveness is not overly helpful in that a variety of definitions exist. Absolute or exclusive definitions are not particularly useful given the contingent nature of managerial effectiveness. The dictionary definition of effectiveness is based on the idea of something or someone achieving its intended purpose. Managers are 'effective' if they fulfil their purpose; but as already discussed, what that purpose is or should be may not always be clear or agreed upon. A look at some of the better-known examples of definitions of managerial effectiveness reveals a range of approaches.

'Efficiency is doing things right, effectiveness is doing the right things right' (Drucker 1967). This definition of Peter Drucker's is the one most commonly cited by other writers in discussing effectiveness. Mintzberg (1983), Kanter (1984) and Peters (1988) all make use of

Drucker's aphorism when making a distinction between 'efficiency', which is defined as optimal or optimum use of resources, and 'effectiveness', which is defined as fulfilling the organisation's purpose. Drucker argues that effectiveness is about achieving results and that these results are to be based on what is right for the business: 'even the most efficient businesses cannot survive, let alone succeed, if it is efficient at doing the wrong thing' (Drucker 1974).

'We define effective managerial behaviour as any set of managerial actions believed to be optimal for identifying, as stimulating, and utilising both internal and external resources toward sustaining over the long term the functioning of the organisation unit for which a manager has some degree of responsibility' (Campbell *et al.* 1970). This definition could be described as more academic and is more complete. However the idea of a clearly defined purpose throughout the organisation is not immediately apparent; it refers primarily to resource utilisation in order to maintain the functioning of the organisation. This could therefore be described as an input and process model rather than output outcome models, i.e. it is more about efficiency than effectiveness.

'There is only one realistic and unambiguous definition of managerial effectiveness. Effectiveness is the extent to which a manager achieves the output requirements of his position. It is the manager's job to be effective, it is his only job' (Reddin 1970). Reddin's approach is fairly blunt, like Drucker's, but it appears to assume that 'output requirements' are always clear and unequivocal.

'Effectiveness is the satisfying of many goals rather than optimising one' (Kirchoff 1977: 348). Kirchoff, whilst being goal-orientated, appears to recognise the multiplicity of demands on and expectations of a manager in terms of the many goals he or she must achieve. This definition could, therefore, be seen as more realistic but it does not give enough emphasis to the need for a clear organisational purpose.

'An effective manager is one who is aware of the different kinds of behaviour and then chooses to engage in those appropriate to the environment, the management job, the situation of his own preferences' (Morse and Wagner 1978: 24). This approach, which was referred to in the previous chapter, is more behavioural and does not mention purpose or achievement; but it does specify compliance with an implicit set of expectations in terms of the way a manager conducts his or herself in the organisation.

'The effective manager is essentially someone who motivates other people and administers resources to ensure that the company's objectives are fulfilled' (Goldsmith and Clutterbuck 1984: 94). This definition incorporates a very traditional approach to the management job, which is about motivating other people and utilising resources. It also clearly recognises that the company – the organisation – has particular objectives which have to be met. However Goldsmith and Clutterbuck were comparing the notion of an 'effective manager' with an 'effective leader' in discussing the need for leadership rather than management in developing winning organisations.

Some earlier studies of managerial effectiveness

In trying to understand managerial effectiveness as seen and defined by other practitioners and academics we come across a number of problems. Firstly, there is little written specifically about managerial effectiveness, although much has been written about managers' jobs, roles, work, leadership, etc. Secondly, much of the research is based on North American work and there are significant cultural and organisational differences which affect the managerial environment of the USA in relation to the UK. Thirdly, apart from some fairly recent work in the last few years, some of which we referred to in Chapter 1, there has not been a great deal of work looking specifically at the public sector and the nature of managerial effectiveness in the public sector in comparison to the private sector.

As suggested above, much ambiguity surrounds the subject of managerial effectiveness and its study. 'Is it managerial work, managerial jobs or managerial behaviour or all of them together?' (Stewart 1989b: 4).

'The fact that managerial work has been analysed so differently reflects not only differences in the research approach but the inherent susceptibility of the phenomena to such diverse analysis' (Hales 1986: 107). Rosemary Stewart suggests that we should perhaps limit ourselves to the terms 'managerial behaviour' and 'managerial jobs', which are easier to operationalise as the subjects of study (Stewart 1989b).

If we accept what appears to be the prevailing definition of effectiveness, i.e. the situational or contingency theory, then managerial effectiveness must be viewed in the context of the individual manager interacting with his or her organisation. Given that managers, when they come into an organisation, occupy a particular job, this would suggest three broad angles from which to examine the question of effectiveness:

1 that of the manager as a person before they enter a particular organisation
2 the particular job they hold in that organisation

3 the factors within the organisational environment influencing or impinging on the manager and his or her reaction to them (the culture).

The manager brings with them a set of experiences, perceptions and skills which have to be tested in and probably adapted to the circumstances of the new organisations. The degree of fit between the individual and the organisation will decide how effective he or she is. Therefore unless a study relates what a manager does to what the organisation requires or expects them to do, it is unlikely to be particularly useful in furthering an understanding of managerial effectiveness. It is important to understand how managers think about their work in an organisation and, in particular, why they think what they think and consequently behave in a particular way.

The manager as a person

Traditionally many attempts to understand the good or effective manager, and what it is that he or she does so that it can be replicated, have centred on the manager as a person and are part of the tradition of studying great leaders and the inherent traits possessed by some individuals, often described as 'charismatic'. A manager may also be a leader but a leader may be no manager. In describing the qualities, characteristics or traits of managers – good or bad – we are immediately faced with the continuing problem of definition and meaning, that is, the problem of defining effectiveness and the words and phrases used to qualify or explain it. This is not an irrelevant semantic or theoretical issue, as the point about leadership in Chapter 2 illustrates.

The problem of the meaning of words used to describe effectiveness is a continuing one and can be illustrated by two studies some 27 years apart. The first one, by Lewis and Stewart (1961), discusses a questionnaire sent by *Fortune* (the American business journal) to 75 top executives. They were asked to indicate the relative importance of 14 qualities. Nearly a third of the respondents felt that all were indispensable – a reflection of the ideal rather than the real? But when asked to describe what they understood by the various trait names, the variety of further descriptions made the use of the terms inoperable for all practical purposes. For example, the word 'dependability' was further described in 147 different ways! A more recent study by Hirsch and Bevan (1988) reviewed how major UK employers describe what they are looking for in managers. They examined where such descriptions came from, whether they were validated and how they were actually used in practice. The information was obtained from the examination of selection, appraisal and training documents plus follow-up interviews. All the different views and phrases were collated into 13 main groups or clusters, with many phrases and descriptions in each of them. Some words such as 'communication' and 'leadership' were more frequently used but the organisations involved stressed the differences in interpretation which exist below the surface of those words. What 'effective communication' means may be culture- and role-specific.

Some studies have also looked at the background and other non-behavioural characteristics that appear to be related to success. For example, Lewis and Stewart (1961) pointed out that private education was a decided advantage in getting to the top in British business. Between one third and one half of British top managers came from private schools, particularly the major private schools. Family connections were also an advantage, especially in smaller- or medium-sized firms; being technically trained, as opposed to having an arts, legal or accounting background, was a distinct advantage. Those who have been successful in business appeared to stay mostly with the same company, which is a characteristic also found by Kotter (1982) in his study of top general managers. An investigation by Kellner and Crowther-Hunt (1980) into the Oxbridge bias in civil service recruitment concluded that it was still marked at that time, in spite of Fulton and the protests of the civil service commission. Recent comments on the civil service suggests that the situation has still not changed radically. Another study in the 1960s, based on getting managers to sort out a list of appropriate adjectives to describe the type of person most likely to succeed as a key executive in top management, produced corresponding lists of the 12 adjectives rated most/least descriptive (Jurgenson 1966). Although this work appeared to be useful it still left the problem of defining what everybody means by a word such as 'productive' when it is used to describe a person most likely to succeed. It can have a number of meanings such as lots of work, producing high quality work or keeping to deadlines. Stewart and Stewart (1981a) point out that in some of their studies Jurgenson's 'least likely to succeed' adjectives were shown to 'characterise the effective manager in a certain firm' (p. 38). The same words or phrases were being used to define opposite qualities.

In 1965 Nash found that there were four roughly identifiable characteristics consistently related to managerial effectiveness at different levels in an organisation. In first-line supervisors and up to middle managers, social science, humanitarian people-orientated interests correlated with effectiveness. With senior managers and upwards the reverse seems to apply. The argument appears to be that at these levels an awareness of others, but without emotional involvement or a focus on an individual benefit, is necessary for manipulating, controlling and organising the organisation as a whole. But Nash also found that at all levels an interest in persuasive, verbal, literary and business pursuits, together with a marked lack of interest in scientific, technical and skilled trade aspects, was related to effectiveness. Nash concluded that there was indicative evidence that effective managers had a wider range of interests, which corroborates with a number of other studies. Wickett and McFarland (1967) found a connection between a diversity of interests at college and later effectiveness in a managerial job.

Another view which has prevailed over the years but is increasingly being questioned is the myth that the well-educated manager with high academic achievement is a natural for success. Peters and Waterman (1982) refer to the analysis paralysis induced by the MBA approach to educating managers. Kotter (1982) in his study of general managers and Bennis and Nanus (1985) in their study of leaders make similar points. Management education does not always lead to applied learning and many such programmes do not help managers to learn how to learn so that they continue to develop and adapt their skills and knowledge to the changing situation. Given the particular turbulence of the public sector discussed in Chapter 1 and the increased emphasis on formal qualifications, this is a particularly important point and is touched on again later.

Motivation has been proposed as a key component of effective management by many researchers and practitioners. Motivation is a complex area with many theories and models. This is put forward as an explanation for different levels of success between two people with similar abilities and strengths, often in the same or very similar organisation environments, for example, McLelland's 'need to achieve' (1962). Lock *et al.* (1978) put forward the view that motivation and ability interact to predict performance. Porter and Lawler's classic (1968) model recognises the complexity of motivation, taking into account a range of variables, including the value of a reward to the individual concerned, the effort/reward probability, the interaction of abilities and traits with the effort required and the perception of role. All these factors come together as determinants of performance. Motivation to succeed may not be the same as being competitive. A study carried out by Helmreich and Spencer (1978) bears this out in that managers with successful careers demonstrated a desire for hard work and interesting and challenging tasks, which was indicative of a drive toward achieving personal standards of excellence irrespective of the opinion of others. Their drive was internal. Equally questionable is the belief that being committed to get to the top is a major determinant of success. Howard (1978) demonstrated that this type of ambition is no longer a prime mover, with more emphasis being placed on the issue of the quality of life; the rounded person who has clear life goals as well as work-related goals is self-confident in their pursuit and consciously maintains a balance between them. In recent years there has been increasing attention given to this issue, not only from a 'quality of working life' standpoint but because of organisations' rejection of a single emphasis on the bottom line. It has become increasingly apparent that by always trying to get the most out of people organisations are not getting the best out of them.

Possession of particular skills, abilities or traits may be indicative of greater potential for success but what really matters is how the manager deploys them in practice in doing his or her job. In other words, can the manager put things together in a way that creates a perception in the minds of others that he or she is useful or valuable to the organisation, and do they want to? Is there only one kind of person who can be successful in a particular context? Are there key skills or attributes which are fundamental to success and, if so, what are they and how applicable are they? Looking at a manager in isolation from his or her organisational context and its demands and expectations is likely to be of very limited use. There would seem to be more value in trying to find out what contributes to effective behaviour in specific organisations and jobs and then seeing what sets of common and particular characteristics emerge. The context defines the effectiveness of managers because it embodies the concepts of purpose, expectations and demands.

The manager's job or role

Various writers have tried to explain and understand the manager in the organisation through focusing either on the role they undertake, the range of behaviours they display, the activities they undertake or the skills they deploy. Many of these descriptions seem to overlap in practice and have the virtue of describing what can be observed. However in doing so, few studies appear to attempt to explain why managers adopt a particular way of behaving in, or 'doing', their particular job.

The term 'role' can be used to describe the point of contact between the manager as an individual person and the organisation. Various studies have attempted to categorise these roles. Levenson (1966) talks about role demands, i.e. what is expected of the occupant of the position in the organisation, and role definition, i.e. the individual's perception of his or her role and its demands and their consequent behaviour in response to their perceptions. Dahrendorf (1968) distinguishes between role behaviour (what the person is expected or required to do), and role attributes (the sort of person the role holder is expected to be). In some of her earlier work Rosemary Stewart (1967) described five different roles or ways of doing a job that the manager might undertake – the emissary, the writer, the discusser, the troubleshooter, the committee man. These were derived from a diary analysis of how managers spent their time. Subsequently she developed this approach through her demands, constraints and choices model (Stewart 1976). Her study of district administrators (Stewart *et al.* 1980) in the National Health Service illustrated how different people do what is apparently the same job differently. These differences are explained in two ways: firstly, in terms of the situational variables derived from the different demands made on each job holder and the different constraints upon action which each job imposes on the holder, together with the choices available to each of the job incumbents; secondly, in terms of their perception of, response to, negotiation of and selection between the demands, constraints and choices of the particular job.

In 1973, Mintzberg analysed real-life managerial incidents to produce a set of ten roles describing the way managers were required to undertake their jobs, depending on the type of job and the organisational position. Three roles, all seen as interpersonal in nature, were figurehead, leader and liaison. The next group was seen as informational: monitor, disseminator and spokesman. The remaining four, entrepreneur, disturbance handler, resource handler and negotiator were seen as decisional roles. These were very much descriptions rather than any attempt to identify what actually led to effective management in a particular context. Morse and Wagner (1978) took a more situational view. Having identified nine managerial roles largely based on the previous work of both Campbell *et al.* (1970) and Mintzberg (1973), they argued that different managers in different jobs, or the same manager at different times and in different situations, placed more or less attention on specific behaviours associated with each one of the nine roles in order to perform effectively.

None of these studies which classify managerial activity roles and activities in this way appear to make any attempt to indicate which type of role or activity is more important to being effective, either directly or by implication. It is their appropriateness to the situation which decides whether or not the manager is effective.

Analysing effectiveness from the standpoint of roles means that any individual manager's effectiveness will be dependent on his or her ability to identify, understand and then act out the appropriate role. Playing a brilliant Hamlet in *King Lear* would not be terribly appropriate! It is not clear how useful a practising manager would find a set of role definitions, coupled to sets of labelled behaviours and activities, as a practical guide to being effective. It would probably be too constraining and artificial and would require interpretation. Its value probably lies mainly in providing a set of general descriptions of managerial activities and behaviours as a basis for practical discussions of what managers do.

An approach developed by Machin (1981), whilst not specifically referring to any particular role definition or performance, produces an 'expectations analysis' focusing on each role incumbent in an organisation. By clarifying and analysing their expectations of each other, a form of multiple role analysis in terms of the collective demands made on each role is constructed. This approach, whilst not providing any ready-made labels, has the particular virtue of being of practical use to managers in a specific organisation. It brings the concepts of roles and analysis down to 'what I expect from you/what you expect from me'.

Assuming a manager has identified what is expected of him or her, by whatever means are appropriate, and he or she is then motivated to want to do something about it, the next stage is then to actually do something. This is perhaps a combination of two sets of factors:

1 being able to make the right choice both in terms of what needs to be done and how, and
2 being able to do it.

Perhaps a useful analogy is that of the golfer who, having identified the demands of the situation in which he or she has to play a shot, not only selects the right club and decides the right way to use it (choice) but is also able to carry out the correct stroke (applied skill/ doing it). Of course some golfers may have a bigger range of clubs than others to choose from, but others may make more skilful use of a smaller range of clubs. Managers as people possess a range of innate skills and abilities; through experience and training they learn to use them and, all being well, extend and develop them.

Katz (1974) outlines three skills a manager must have: technical, human and conceptual. These are related to organisational levels. Technical skill is detailed practical and theoretical knowledge of a specific field which the manager is able to apply, e.g. the specific technical and professional skills of the personnel manager or financial manager. These technical skills are usually needed at lower levels in large organisations and throughout smaller ones. Human skills encompass managing and leading groups and the relations between groups, which is increasingly needed as a manager moves up the hierarchy. Conceptual skill is about implementing corporate strategy and seeing the organisation holistically in terms of its priorities, conflicts, probabilities and changing patterns. Burgoyne and Stewart (1976) identify 11 skills related to three different types of learning: learning facts, learning different responses and learning to conceptualise. These seem to correspond to Katz's three skills in a number of ways. The work of Harry Schroeder (1989) on his 11 high performance competencies is similar in that he identifies these as the highest of three levels of competency. The first relates to the effectiveness of the individual in interacting with others, and the second is concerned with technical/ professional skills. The high performance competencies encompass higher order conceptual and interactive capabilities that higher performing managers display and which can be developed.

The grouping of skills developed by Burgoyne and Stewart is based on research into the attributes possessed by successful managers and relates to how managers learn about their jobs and how to be effective in them. Many studies seem to ignore this vital aspect of a manager's learning: how to manage the nature of their managerial job and the organisational context in which they work in order to keep pace with the changes in the work environment and the wider environment in which the organisation exists. Writers such as Revans, Argyris and Schon, Burgoyne and Pedlar are among the few who explicitly recognise the Darwinian nature of individual managerial effectiveness and the need for constant learning, change and adaptation.

Revans first referred to organisations as learning systems in 1969. His ideas about action learning (Revans 1982) are expressed in the conclusion that learning needs to be greater than or at least equal to the rate of change on both an individual and organisation level, if both individuals and the organisation are to continue to be effective. Argyris and Schon's ideas (1978) form the basis of much of the current thinking about the 'learning organisation', which has been adopted particularly by people like Pedler *et al.* (1991), Garratt (1991) and Senge (1992). These ideas include the concept of 'double loop learning.' According to this idea, both individuals and organisation not only continually learn how to do better things they already do, they also initiate learning about how to do new things. The new things are in response to looking upward and outward into the wider environment in which they work. For individuals this may be seeing their particular job or department in the context of the whole organisation. For the organisation – its top managers – this may be the external context and market in which it operates. This reading of the wider context leads to a reframing of thinking about the relevance of what is being done and how it is being done and of the process of learning itself. The outcome may be a radical change in the nature of the organisation.

Burgoyne (1976) postulates how a manager interacts with the organisation environment through carrying out 'inner plans' or programmes with a particular purpose in mind, which he or she then modifies in response to feedback from the organisation environment. Effectiveness is then a combination of the fit of the plans and purposes to each other and to the situation, which is determined by the possession of the skills identified in their study and the ability to apply them in practice. This sensitivity to the situation in which the manager works seems to be particularly important in translating other innate or learning skills and attributes into something useful – effective – in any organisation.

Some managers seem intuitively to be able to make the right choice about what is important for them to do in a particular organisational context in order to be considered effective. What has often been referred to as 'intuition' has in more recent years been more deeply understood as a particular cognitive process. Agor (1985) conducted a survey of top American executives who used intuition as a tool in guiding their decision making. Managers increasingly have to make decisions in a climate characterised by rapid and discontinuous change. Rational left brain thinking and the use of linear models based on past trends are likely to be increasingly inaccurate or misleading. Research into right brain thinking is demystifying the skills and processes involved in 'intuition' and shows how they can be developed and applied. This echoes the difference between P and Q learning described by Revans (1982), the former being programmed learning based on knowledge gleaned from past experience whereas the latter represent a questioning process to produce insights into new problems. Peters and Waterman (1982) reported that the ten best companies encouraged the use of intuitive skills and nurtured its development in their management culture. Stamp (1986) discusses the growing disenchantment with a purely analytic style of management, pointing out that 'the most highly skilled analysts are not usually to be found in key line roles' (p. 27). The analytic approach enhances the skill of ordering alternatives from which choices might be made but inhibits the ability of the manager to identify what the problems are in the first place. Stamp cites a number of writers who suggest that 'the exclusively analytic approach must be complemented by a new valuing of intuition' (p 27) and goes on to link this to the development and understanding of left brain/right brain information processing.

Sisson and Storey (1988), in discussing the development of effective managers, describe the situation where an increasing number of organisations demand managers who are able to break out of the organisation's routine and demonstrate behaviour of characteristics associated with innovation enterprise. However, according to Sisson and Storey, there still appeared to be some organisations where this characteristic would be inappropriate and would lead to ineffective managerial performance because the smooth administration of the system remains the overriding requirement. Sisson and Storey emphasise that the one thing organisations ignore at their peril is to seek and produce some definition of what they expect their managers to do, however difficult this may be to achieve.

The organisational environment

It is difficult to separate out the innate skills, characteristics or attributes of a particular person who fulfils a managerial role from the nature of that role or particular job in an organisation. This is because all of these factors overlap with each other in producing an effective managerial outcome. The organisational context or situation is not an isolated feature but is both produced by and conditions the behaviour of the managers in the organisation – the culture of the organisation. Managerial effectiveness is a contingent or situational concept. It is elusive and dependent on time, context and the evaluating audience (Pye 1988). It seems there can be no absolute definition or concept of managerial effectiveness. It is a function of who defines it (Lombardo and McCall 1982). In 1976 Burgoyne pointed out that a contingent or situational definition of effectiveness can result in a particularism in that managerial effectiveness can only be defined in terms of particular managers in particular organisations at a particular point in time. The work of Stewart and Stewart (1981a) firmly supports this view. They do not put forward a general theory of effectiveness but instead advance a number of propositions that should be considered by anyone seeking to investigate managerial effectiveness. They suggest:

- Behaviour which is effective in one country cannot be assumed to be effective in another, even in the same firm.
- The requirements for effective management may differ greatly between different levels of management, even in the same firm.
- The requirements for effective management in one firm may be vastly different from the requirements for effective management in another firm.
- Some of this difference may be due to differences in product or

service, some to size; some to geographical dispersion and some to the history and internal politics of the firm.
- What people say constitutes effective management may be different from their behaviour when actually judging and promoting people and what people say about their own management style may be very different from the way they behave.
- Empirical studies of what, at present, is regarded as effective management may yield information which is surprising or unwelcome. This information is ignored at one's peril.

(Stewart and Stewart: 1981a)

As referred to in Chapter 2, Stewart and Stewart found between 60 and 90 characteristics to differentiate the effective from the ineffective manager, a third of these remaining stable across organisations and jobs. The remaining two-thirds reflected the particular nature of the job organisation, etc. They described some of the more general characteristics of the effective manager as:

- giving people credit for good work
- protecting them in public
- delegating to them the challenging rather than the donkey work
- developing one or more subordinates so that they are ready to take the manager's place
- viewing his or her information, decisions, etc. from the point of view of their effect on the organisation as a whole in the long term.

The helicopter approach exemplified in the last point was particularly considered to be the sign of an effective manager at senior level.

Many of the studies devoted specifically to the issue of managerial effectiveness appear to emphasise a situational particularism, i.e. that it must be defined for the particular job and organisation in question. Some factors, however, will probably be common especially when looking at similar jobs within the same organisational culture. It could also be said that there is an inherent paradox in managerial effectiveness in that whilst each situation is relatively unique and each manager is relatively unique, the state of effectiveness is achieved only if there is congruence between these two uniquenesses. A manager can bring about congruence by either meeting the expectations as given, or if the necessary skills are not at hand, then attempting to renegotiate or re-educate others so that the set of expectations are those that the manager is able to meet. He or she either adapts themselves to the situation or adapts the situation to suit themselves; either way particular skills or abilities are required. The following points may perhaps help clarify and summarise:

1 there are situationally specific expectations that cannot be ignored
2 each job in each situation requires a different blend of skills and attributes, though there are some common ones
3 there are some personal attributes or skills that suggest one person is more likely to be an effective manager than another
4 different managers, with different combinations of skills, attributes and experience, can achieve equal success if they are situationally sensitive, i.e. they can identify correctly what is expected of them in the organisational situation and also:

- have the appropriate blend of skills and attributes to meet the expectations as they stand or
- have the capacity to renegotiate expectations so that they are achievable with their particular blend of skills or
- can adapt their skills and attributes, through self-awareness and the capacity to learn, to meet the expectations as they stand or
- can combine elements of all the above three.

Hales (1986) criticises some of the studies of managerial effectiveness, and is backed up in this by Rosemary Stewart (1989b), because there appears to have been a reluctance to treat managers' observable behaviours as problematic and to ask (or keep asking) the question 'why these behaviours and activities?' It is suggested that managers' internal view of their organisational world derives from the experience of working in the organisation, i.e. what seems to work or be acceptable provides the basic reason why they behave in a particular way. The attribute or skill of situational sensitivity seems to be an underlying key factor in achieving a congruence between expectations and behaviour, i.e. effectiveness. If the manager lacks this key factor of situational sensitivity, then no matter what range of other skills they possess they are unlikely to be able to identify correctly the expectations held of them and therefore they will not be able to behave congruently.

A simple model of managerial effectiveness, which attempts to pull together some of the factors involved under the three headings of the person, job and organisation, is illustrated in Figure 3.1.

Figure 3.1 A model of managerial effectiveness
Managers must be able to read their situations accurately. The
situation is made up of three factors: the person, job and organisation.
Managers need to be sensitive to them in order to understand which
job-related behaviours will fit, i.e. be congruent with the organisational
context.

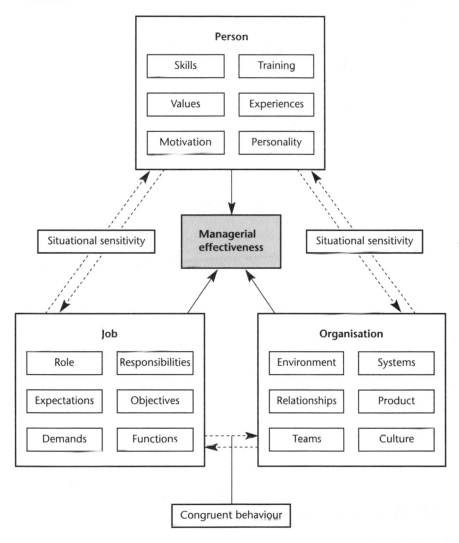

| Chapter | | **How managers develop**
| four | | **their model of**
| | | **managerial effectiveness**

Managers and their staff assess each other's performance whether or not there is any formal system for doing so. It is an instinctive process. Decisions about individuals, which affect their jobs and careers and the performance of the organisation, are made on the basis of these assessments. All organisations have a 'performance culture', i.e. a set of beliefs and norms of behaviour which affect its performance, for better or worse.

Both experience and research suggest that 'effective performance appraisal in organisations continues to be a compelling but unrealisable goal' (Banks and Murphy 1985: 335). For example, a manager may have two subordinates who have achieved all their work objectives to pre-agreed performance standards, but one is perceived to perform more effectively than the other. Why is this? What is it that the senior manager has in mind that leads to the view that one of the subordinates is better than the other? Can it be made explicit? If it can, why is it not set out as a performance objective? Does the other manager know that he or she is not meeting this particular criterion of success?

Problems with selection, training and development and individual performance review occur in a number of areas and there is much advice available on how to overcome these problems. But the most difficult area seems to be defining and articulating what actually constitutes effective performance, namely:

• what precisely is it we are assessing?
• what is it we actually expect of our managers?

- can this be expressed comprehensively and in detail?
- how does it differ between people and jobs?
- how does it relate to and affect the performance of an organisation as a whole?

The criteria being applied in managerial processes to do with selecting, developing and appraising managers are critical to the success of the organisation and must be made explicit so that they can be examined and interrogated in terms of their effect on both short- and long-term organisational performance.

This chapter examines the issues that affect how we define the effective manager or effective performance from the point of view of having to carry out the selection, development and appraisal of others. It examines the factors that govern how we develop a view of effective managerial performance, and in particular, how we arrive at an assessment about the performance of others.

Expectations of effective performance

The problem is that most of us have a perception of what effective managerial performance is but we may not have thought it through sufficiently to articulate it to ourselves, let alone communicate clearly to others.

As discussed earlier, there is a widely held view that management effectiveness is contingent, derived from what others expect or require managers to do. 'Good or bad practice may be conceived in terms of the extent to which managers' performance matches others' expectations' (Hales 1986: 108) and 'effectiveness is a multi-determined entity depending on the manager, his position, the organisation and the socio-economic environment' (Langford 1979: 34). It would seem that effectiveness, therefore, should not be taken as some objective absolute which holds good for all managerial jobs in all organisations. Whilst there may be similarities, effectiveness can be defined only in situational terms, i.e. 'What do you expect of me in my job in this business unit or organisation?'

A manager's effectiveness cannot be assessed in a recruitment process or improved through training and appraisal until it is clear as to what constitutes a particular view of effectiveness and what criteria are being used, explicitly or implicitly, to assess it. The description of a manager as effective in practice may have as its inspiration aspects of the manager's personality, his/her relationship with seniors and peers, major tasks or objectives achieved, or a combination of these and other factors. Different organisational contexts and circumstances may dictate whether a particular manager is viewed as successful or not at any point in time. An effective manager in one organisation may be judged as less effective in another. Managers have to reconcile a range of competing objectives and expectations between superiors, peers and subordinates and may be assessed as both effective and ineffective at the same time by subordinates and superiors. Such discrepancies may say as much about the organisational culture and values, in terms of its ability to communicate to managers what is expected of them, as about the manager's ability to recognise what needs to be done to be judged as effective.

To be effective, a manager must be able to match the requirements of the situation in which he or she works. They may well have the skills to recognise and meet expectations, adapting as necessary. Equally, it may well be chance that brings about a match between expectations and performance. If circumstances change, for example a change of job or a change in the management style or culture owing to a take-over or reorganisation, it may result in a mismatch. This emphasises the contingent or situational nature of effectiveness. In other words, effectiveness is dependent upon the situation. The situation incorporates the person who is the manager, the position or job, the organisation and its environment. A key skill must be the ability to read accurately the demands and expectations of the situation, irrespective of whether they are explicit or implicit. If a manager misreads their situation there will be a performance gap. However, if they read it accurately but the organisational environment is encouraging albeit unwittingly an inappropriate view of managerial effectiveness, there will be a negative performance effect for the organisation.

Developing a personal concept of effectiveness

Most of the descriptions and definitions of managerial effectiveness and leadership discussed in Chapter 3 have been proffered by academics and researchers as a result of formal studies of managers at work. Practising managers have minimal opportunity to study themselves and others in action, so how do they arrive at a concept of managerial effectiveness? To what extent is it made explicit and shared, and does it consciously guide their behaviour and approach to their job?

A manager behaves in a particular way based on his or her experiences of working in a particular organisation. Managers invest in models of the reality of their organisational life which help them understand and anticipate what is going on (Beck 1980). All managers' models of the organisation may not be the same, but it is probable that some of them will overlap. The degree of overlap will be dependent on the extent to which models are shared, discussed and evaluated. For example, through sharing views about effectiveness and what needs to be done by managers to be effective, through various management education and development processes and in establishing a basis for selection and appraisal. As we have seen there may also be a problem in sharing the meaning of the words used to discuss aspects of managerial work and the managerial activities and behaviour they represent.

It is important for anyone involved in assessing others to have some insight into how he or she arrives at such an assessment, how his or her perception of what constitutes effective management has been developed and how he or she processes information about another person. For example, a manager appraising his or her staff will bring to the process a personal and possibly unconscious view of what constitutes effective performance, which may or may not coincide with the views of others in the organisation. His or her experiences will have led to a particular way of construing managerial effectiveness.

Kelly's (1955) theory of personal constructs referred to earlier explains the often marked difference in how people see, interpret and act in relation to both the same and different events and people. People are constantly formulating, testing and, if necessary, revising their views about the world they inhabit. Each person's processes are psychologically channelised by the way in which they anticipate events.

Kelly's personal construct theory explains how a person develops a set of perceptions or views about the world he or she inhabits. Kelly's model is of a person as a scientist exploring their environment and developing hypotheses derived from experience, formulating, testing and if necessary revising a series of propositions or laws about the world they inhabit. These propositions or hypotheses are unique to each individual and derive from his or her personal experience of the world or part of it, e.g. the organisational context in which a manager works. These experience-derived hypotheses not only reflect experience but come to influence behaviour and condition expectations. Some models may be 'better' than others if they help each person to understand their world more accurately and anticipate a wider range of events. The better a manager's model of the organisation the more likely he or she is to be able to be effective in that organisation. They will be situationally sensitive.

Kelly describes a person's system or model as a 'construct system' 'because the word "construct" carries with it both the sense of having being constructed or developed from experience and also the sense of being that through which we construe – or see and interpret – the world' (Stewart and Stewart 1981b). Understanding someone's construct system helps us to understand his or her experiences and to know something about what a particular situation is likely to mean to that person. Kelly divided the thoughts we have into two parts. *Elements* refer to the person, object, activity, event or situation upon which thoughts are focused. *Constructs* are the views or feelings about, or qualities ascribed to, the element. Constructs tend to be interlinked; some have greater importance than others. The technique that Kelly developed for making these constructions explicit so that they could be consciously examined or explored is known as the *repertory grid*. In essence, this involves getting people to identify a number of elements in the area to be examined, for example personal relationships, career choices or managerial effectiveness, and then asking them to describe the various characteristics or qualities they ascribe to them, namely their constructs. In focusing on managerial effectiveness in a particular organisation, the elements could be a range of managers whom the interviewee considers to be effective or ineffective, without initially attempting to establish any criteria for selection, other than the interviewee's perception of them as effective or ineffective. Then by following a particular method of comparing and contrasting the managers, the constructs used by the interviewee to think about effectiveness are brought out. This produces one view of what constitutes managerial effectiveness. The results of a range of similar interviews can be compared by various means, subject to certain conditions of limitations, to see if there is any similarity.

In looking at managerial effectiveness in an organisation, individual managers are unlikely to have exactly the same view of what sort of behaviour constitutes effective managerial performance unless there has been some rigorous work undertaken to make explicit, to share and to understand the dimensions of effectiveness that are important, or believed to be important in the organisation. Unless there are clear unequivocal and understood organisational performance dimensions, which the manager feels able to meet, and which form part of both the individual and collective construct system (the organisational culture), each manager will operate on the basis of his or her own personal experience. Their own personal construct systems will be the major influence on their behaviour (Kelly 1955; Bannister and Fransella 1971; Stewart and Stewart 1981b).

It has already been suggested that public sector organisations face a particular problem in establishing clear performance dimensions on an organisation-wide basis. Therefore to find out what managers believe constitutes effective managerial behaviour we need to find out the criteria, dimensions or characteristics they use that influence both their own behaviour and lead them to view others as effective or otherwise. What are the expectations each manager holds of all the other managers, which if met lead to a perception of effectiveness – either real or reputational? What are their perceptions of the match between actual and expected behaviour? What labels are put on the behaviours that lead to a judgement of effective/non-effective?

Categorisation is basic to perception and to information storage and organisation (Feldman 1981). Categorisation can be described as 'the process of classifying stimuli into categories composed of traits or prototypes' (Dunn *et al.* 1987: 16). Given the vast amount of often contradictory information we receive about people (and everything else around us) categorisation is a means of simplifying perceptions and the storage and organisation of the information on which our perceptions are based. The categories we use are unlikely to be very clearly defined, particularly if they have not been deliberately made explicit, identified and examined. Feldman (1981) describes one person as perceiving another in terms of categories which are 'fuzzy sets defined by family resemblance among their members and exemplified by category prototypes or images . . . the specific category to which they are assigned is a function of perceiver and situational factors' (p. 130).

If managers can describe these categories as effective/non-effective, and articulate the words and phrases used to describe the forms of behaviour that cause them to assign managers to one or other category, we can begin both to understand the factors that managers in a particular organisation believe constitute effective or ineffective behaviour and to develop a communication about it using their terminology. Knowing how their managers believe they ought to behave must be of considerable value to an organisation in terms of its future survival and success. What are the consequences for the organisation of the way managers believe they should behave in order to be effective, in terms of its ability to achieve its purpose or even its survival?

Another difficulty, in both defining effectiveness and in examining the constructs and categories from which it is built up, is that of sharing the meanings of the words used. In its full form, a repertory grid allows detailed exploration both of the meanings of words and phrases and the ideas, experiences, concepts and qualities they act as a vehicle for. In conducting grid interviews, constructs are developed and explored with the interviewees but there is a limit to which this can be done, because of both the time involved and the extent to which it is legitimate to push and probe personal views and perceptions.

Hannabuss (1987: 34–9) discusses the essential need to clarify and negotiate meanings in management and the way that organisations develop a set of meanings which are culturally derived and shared. 'The culture is one of shared networks of meanings, of agreed methods of doing things (e.g. contractual bondings, tacit concessions to power, coping strategies with conflict, perceptions of valid rewards) which guide scripts of human behaviour' (p. 35).

Managers spend a large part of their time talking, out of which meanings are clarified and developed. Management is 'a social collective whose members have a set of implicit and explicit meanings acquired through innumerable communicative exchanges' (Gowler and Legge 1983: 198). The quality and quantity of these exchanges will probably vary according to such factors as the opportunity for contact and exchange, the degree to which such sharing and communication is the norm and the degree to which there is a common base of managerial knowledge and theory.

Hannabuss discusses Drucker's (1967) book *The Effective Executive*, describing the way in which the meaning of the word 'effectiveness' is built up by Drucker in laying out before the reader his particular understanding of the concept of effectiveness. Hannabuss also underlines the importance of 'the reader's own semantic memory and active cognitive processes' (Hannabuss 1987: 36), which categorise and order the information they receive.

'Distinguishing information and differentiating it in category form (from A and not A opposites to more complex taxonomies) is a central part of all learning' (Hannabuss 1987: 36). It is a process which occurs both in the mind of the reader and of the authors, who make explicit their thought processes through the pages of this book. The reader/ managers and authors/researchers category systems come into contact, resulting either in the reader's set of categories and constructs being altered by the authors, or the reader experiencing such a degree of cognitive dissonance that he or she finds it difficult to accept and use the meanings, and therefore the arguments, definitions and explanations proffered by the authors in defining the reader's own concept of effectiveness.

Collecting and processing accurate
information on the effectiveness of others

All management processes to do with assessing others require information. For example, Feldman (1981) discusses this in relation to appraisal. The ability and willingness of the appraiser to collect information is fundamental to the success of the process and will depend on a number of factors, such as training in appropriate appraisal skills, his or her understanding of the system and its purpose and the availability of information about appraisees within the organisational context. Awareness of how we as individuals collect and process information about each other in the normal course of events can help overcome some of the in-built preconceptions.

The contact managers have with their staff is often fleeting and confined to particular situations. *Direct* information about *all* aspects of the job done by a subordinate and their actual behaviour in carrying it out is therefore limited in most job situations. Jobs, particularly at senior level, may be specified only in general terms and subject to varying interpretations and expectations. The context in which a manager has to obtain information for appraisal has been described as an 'uncertain, informationally noisy environment' against which the manager 'must perform several cognitive tasks before performance appraisals are possible' (Feldman 1981: 128). These mental tasks constitute the following:

1 recognise and consider relevant information about the person being appraised
2 mentally organise and store this information for later use, probably integrating it with existing information
3 be able to recall and use the information in an organised way when required, e.g. when allocating work
4 be able, when required, e.g. because of need to undertake a formal appraisal, to integrate all the information into some form of summary judgement.

The performance appraisal process is therefore a complex and cyclical process or combination of interacting processes concerned with the acquisition, ordering and recall of information about an employee's behaviour at work. There are both personal and organisational factors working against the efficiency and effectiveness of the process.

The mental tasks described above refer to the way information is processed, i.e. recognised, categorised, stored, recalled and finally integrated into a performance assessment. Fundamental to this is the system of categories which is used by managers to handle the information they receive and hold about their staff.

People react, often unconsciously, to certain cues in other people's behaviour or appearance which help to place them in particular categories to which are attributed certain characteristics. At its most basic this could be man/woman or black/white. In a managerial context a person may be classified as a team worker, high achiever or poor leader. In some organisations such as the National Health Service there is a particular tendency to classify people according to the professional or occupational group (the tribe) to which they belong or from which they have come, e.g. nurse, finance manager, personnel manager, doctor or chief executive. This leads to the assumption that certain characteristics are possessed by individuals in this category, even if there is no direct experience of them. The effect of categorisation on performance evaluation is to 'limit and select information about the employee when memory-based judgements are made' (Feldman 1981: 140).

Even when conscious effort is made to confirm impressions by obtaining and using information about performance with an objectives-based system, it seems that expected or anticipated forms of behaviour are noticed and recalled more than the unexpected, even when information about both is equally available. Categorisation therefore not only selectively influences and biases recall, it prevents contradictory evidence from appearing and, in fact, elicits confirming evidence.

What this means is that once a manager is assigned to a category prototype by his/her boss, or anyone else, the recall of information about him or her will be biased towards the category prototype. In other words, the manager will be assumed to possess the characteristics of the category in which he/she has been placed. Even when there is hard information to the contrary on the employee's actual behaviour it will tend to be used selectively, especially when it has to be recalled from memory. If a manager is perceived as a go-getter, fast-track management trainee or personnel manager, etc. he or she is likely to have his/her work behaviour interpreted and recalled less in terms of what was actually done than in terms of what a 'typical' go-getter, etc. is presumed, by the assessor, to do. The increasing popularity of peer/subordinate appraisal, partly induced by the decline of traditional managerial hierarchies in many organisations, provides a wider range of information and therefore raises accuracy in the sense of a commonality of impression. However the same set of problems apply.

When appraisal decisions about employees are made, information has to be retrieved from memory. As described earlier, our memory is biased towards the category or stereotype to which we first assigned the employee, which in turn is based on our construction of our world. Any searching of our memory is therefore conditioned towards the information that fits the category stereotype. In fact the information we have collected along the way is filtered by the category traits. If we have initially seen someone as intellectual rather than practical, i.e. categorised him/her as an intellectual, we will accept information that supports this but tend to ignore or filter out contrary information, e.g. demonstrations of practical ability.

If we have ample opportunity to see an employee at work in all aspects of his or her work then we may be able to acquire sufficient real information about them to correct any miscategorisation or over-simplified categorisation. But there is another set of problems inherent in getting this information, which was touched on earlier.

Any appraisal system requires that a manager appraising their staff needs information about their work performance. The problems inherent in the process of acquiring information have been pointed out. In practical terms a manager has to rely on his or her own knowledge of an employee. That knowledge needs to be based on observing what an employee actually does, not on what the manager thinks he or she does.

Observation of job behaviour is critical for appraisal reliability and validity (Banks and Murphy 1985: 335–45). Observation can be defined as opportunities to acquire first-hand information about how and what a subordinate is doing. It needs to be frequent, unbiased and properly representative of the range of the employee's work and behaviour.

Many individual performance review schemes refer to the need for regular and frequent information review discussions which are open, positive, supportive and forward looking so that the performance review is not a once-a-year event. But 'observation in organisations is fraught with distortion and inadequacies: observation is infrequent and noisy and appraisers lack focus owing to competing pressures, motivation and demands' (p. 341). Managers might benefit from training not only in how to observe in these circumstances, but probably more importantly in how to decide what to observe. They need to determine what aspects of performance are measurable, i.e. can be observed validly, against a description or set of expectations of effective performance. They should attempt to develop 'a prototype . . . a specific coherent behavioural definition of satisfactory or superior performance . . . what the typical satisfactory or superior worker DOES' (p. 342).

The difficulty of sharing meanings and accepting and internalising them is potentially difficult enough in a situation where meaning and definition are carefully argued, clarified and built up. It must be even more difficult in an organisational context where managers are likely to have different meanings for commonly used words and may be struggling to understand why they hold different views about the effectiveness of a colleague, the selection of a new manager or why appraisals or individual performance reviews can produce such different assessments. 'Just because an expression is widely used we should not be fooled into thinking that its meaning is understood consistently across organisations, or even within them?' (Hirsch and Bevan 1988: 11). The same manager may be classed as effective or non-effective at the same time by different people in an organisation using either the same or different factors depending on how they personally construe 'effectiveness'. Kelly and others (Bannister and Fransella 1971) have described how individuals vary, not only because they have different constructs which they use to categorise different people in situations, but because they use different factors or constructs to categorise the same situation or person.

In conclusion, when considering the concept of effectiveness that individual managers develop, there are three basic issues:

1 the difficulty of individual managers articulating the nature of mana-gerial effectiveness as they perceive it in a particular organisation
2 the individual and collective problem of understanding it and why or how it has been arrived at
3 finding a language for sharing and communicating it.

Assuming it has managed to cope with these three issues, an organi-sation is then faced with the fact that this is the form of behaviour it is expecting or perhaps conditioning (albeit not intentionally) its managers to adopt. It has to deal with the consequences of this view which may or may not be considered appropriate. This is not to imply that managers have no influence over the development of 'expecta-tions' or over their own behaviour. They do, especially if they are in more senior and influential jobs in the organisation. The problem may be that those managers who can influence behaviour and expec-tations are often themselves unaware of what they are.

A practical example of these issues is described in Chapter 7, which discusses an empirical examination of individual effectiveness.

Chapter	**Organisational cultures**
five	**and models of**
	effectiveness

All organisations have a discernible culture. It is the effect of the totality of all the organisation's artefacts. Culture is not a separate factor like the balance sheet. In some cases the nature of the culture, and certain of its artefacts, are much more clearly identifiable and powerful in their effect on individuals and on performance.

The organisation's culture is both a product of and a shaper of individual behaviour. Many organisations devote considerable effort to creating and maintaining a particular culture that consciously reinforces explicit messages in order to encourage and support particular forms of behaviour that it believes are important. These may have evolved from past success and reflect that experience in replicating associated ways of doing things. Arguably, in the majority of organisations, culture may be more a product of freely interacting factors or limited intervention so that messages received by people in the organisation are implicit, weak or contradictory. This could be because of a number of reasons, such as powerful professional subcultures which promote factional rather than corporate interests, diffuse leadership or uncertainty over priorities and what actually constitutes success.

The organisation's model of effectiveness

In terms of individual managerial effectiveness, the critical factor is that all organisations do have a collective but usually implicit view of effectiveness. The research undertaken in the NHS discussed later, in Chapter 7, underlines this. Even in similar organisations within the same sector there are common elements but significant differences. A manager's perception of what constitutes effective management behaviour is conditioned by their experience of the organisation. That experience governs both their own behaviour and their expectations of others. The effect of that experience may be to downgrade individual and organisational performance if either the 'wrong' message is given or if it is read incorrectly. There is a self-reinforcing loop of experience in organisations which perpetuates behaviour. To understand the effect of this, the collective picture of effectiveness derived from each individual manager must be made explicit so that it can be interrogated, and then action taken to either reinforce or change all managers' experience of the organisation. The essential questions to be addressed are:

- how is managerial effectiveness viewed in practice by managers at all levels, i.e. what are their beliefs about what constitutes effective management performance?
- how does this view, whether held consciously or unconsciously, affect their approach to the selection, assessment/appraisal and development of subordinates, i.e. the perpetuation of the cultural model of effectiveness?
- what is the effect on organisational performance of the practical application of these beliefs, i.e. the cumulative effect of management activity?

The cultural context of the model

The literature and research on the nature of successful organisations seems to reach a number of similar conclusions on the key components of success, which could be summarised as follows:

1 all successful organisations developed a clearly articulated and understood mission or vision which clarified the purpose of the organisation
2 they developed a coherent strategy or integrated set of strategies for the achievement of that mission
3 both points 1 and 2 must be clearly and consistently communicated to the people who are going to make it happen
4 all the above three points must be built on and reflect a set of values that makes people believe they are important to and respected by the organisation.

5 all the above four points require leadership to bring them into being and to maintain them.

Whichever of the 'big ideas' of the last 15 years (e.g. quality, performance management, human resource management, the learning organisation) one examines, these component factors reoccur as issues to be addressed. The last case, that of the learning organisation, makes more explicit a sixth factor. Though not fundamentally new, it is now recognised as increasingly important in relation to organisational success and survival. *Adaptability* is based on the capacity of the firm or organisation to be constantly learning about its own (changing) environment and the effectiveness and efficiency of its structure, strategies, policies and processes in relation to that environment and adapt or replace them accordingly.

Kotter and Heskett (1992) conducted four studies of American firms and also looked in some detail at ICI under (Sir) John Harvey-Jones 'to determine whether a relationship exists between corporate culture and long-term economic performance' (p. 10). They concluded that:

1 corporate culture can have a significant impact on a firm's long-term economic performance
2 corporate culture will probably be an even more important factor in determining the success or failure of firms in the next decade
3 corporate cultures that inhibit strong long-term financial performance are not rare; they develop easily, even in firms that are full of reasonable and intelligent people
4 although tough to change, corporate culture can be made more performance-enhancing.

As always with findings and examples drawn from North American and private sector organisations, there are issues of transferability in relation to different contexts. The UK context is different to the USA and, as discussed in Chapter 1, there is increasing understanding of some of the real differences between public and private sector organisations. However, it is hard to ignore the weight of evidence that now exists about the impact of the organisation's culture on the behaviour of individuals in the organisation and therefore, ultimately, on its performance and outcomes. There may be less certainty about the nature of an appropriate management culture in public sector organisations and about how to change it in order to improve performance and outcomes, but it is nevertheless a critical issue. The culture of an organisation exists and can be described, irrespective of whether or not it has been created and managed. This culture both produces and is an amalgam of the varying beliefs and expectations of the people in it. An individual manager senses, with varying degrees of accuracy, the range of expectations others in his or her role set have of him/her, particularly those of more senior managers who are seen as influential exemplars. An unmanaged culture produces an unmanaged set of expectations. The manager may then selectively negotiate, ignore, or respond to those they feel are most important to them. The judgement about what is most important is likely to be highly subjective and based on their assumptions about what will affect personal survival and success in their particular environment.

Returning to Kotter and Heskett (1992), they point out that it is not strong and well-defined cultures *per se* that produce high performance, because they can encourage even intelligent people, who may have good information and ideas about an assumed context and environment based on past success, to behave destructively unless the culture also contains values and norms of behaviour that can help organisations adapt to a changing environment.

Kotter and Heskett define leadership by top managers as critical to driving the creation of an appropriate culture, which is then passed on to all existing and new managers. Passing it on needs to be a conscious and deliberate process. Top managers have to motivate senior and middle managers 'to play a similar kind of leadership role in creating change for their own divisions, departments and groups' (p. 146). The time-scale for new cultures to emerge and bed in is 10 to 15 years, very much a long-distance race. There has been a major and sustained push to change the culture of public sector organisations in the UK since 1980. But as Williams (1985) wrote in *Better Management, Better Health* when discussing the emerging management culture in the NHS: 'In the NHS the managerial culture of the service is less clear and confident than it is in the best industrial organisations' (p. 6). The position of the NHS and many other public sector organisations is not much changed today. We are still uncertain about adopting private sector methods in public sector organisations and political time-scales are far shorter than those needed for enabling a real and appropriate cultural shift.

Creating appropriate expectations

The psychologist B. F. Skinner (1953) stated that 'the behavior that gets rewarded gets repeated'. All change in organisations is dependent on one or more people being prepared to work differently to the way they currently do. Managerial behaviour is critical to driving an organisation in a particular direction: so what behaviours on the part of managers actually get rewarded – directly or, possibly more importantly, indirectly? The existing culture will be a product of the behaviours that have been rewarded in the past.

The public sector changes have produced a different environment that rewards different forms of managerial behaviour than previously. The rewards are less clear, though, than in many private sector organisations. As suggested above, there is an uncertainty about what is appropriate behaviour. Stewart and Walsh (1992) describe a number of key factors characterising the change in the management of public services, including both the separation of the political process from the managerial and a change of culture. Pollitt (1993) uses the term 'managerialism' to encompass these changes, referring to a 'set of beliefs and practices, at the core of which burns the seldom tested assumption that better management will prove an effective solvent for a wide range of economic and social ills' (p. 81). The environment for public sector managers is giving an unclear message. Expectations are many and conflicting.

Thompson *et al.* (1994), in a study of the approach to human resource management in NHS trusts as a result of public sector changes, describe 'a set of values characterised by an authoritarian and increasingly instrumental or new Taylorist orientation . . .' (p. 31) akin to McGregor's (1960) theory 'X'. The views of 34 top managers (chief executives and human resource directors) were obtained and clearly demonstrated much more of a business orientation, particularly on the part of the CEOs. But the top managers also stated the view that they and their business are having to operate in an increasingly threatening environment. There is a greater perception of personal threat in terms of increased personal accountability where failure will be punished rather than success rewarded. Public sector changes do not seem to be perceived as a liberating devolution and delegation of real authority. Of course there are threatening cultures in private sector organisations which result in similar perceptions of personal threat by top managers. These may be externally derived – competitors, declining product markets, etc. – or they may be a result of internal organisational values and norms, where the prevailing approach to any perceived weakness or failure is predatory. However it seems that a saving factor in private sector organisations is that leaders can emerge or be appointed with endowed or negotiated wide-ranging powers to make changes in a way that cannot be duplicated in many public sector organisations. The issue of public accountability requires 'goldfish bowl' management to an extent that would not be expected or tolerated in many private sector organisations. The limitations imposed on leaders in the public sector by political processes, public accountability and the short-term nature of public sector planning, performance and financial cycles make it difficult to see how internally driven culture change can be effected so easily in public sector organisations.

(Sir) John Harvey-Jones (1992) in the British *Troubleshooter* television series commented on some of the differences he experienced between public and private sector organisations. The series had not intended to deal with public sector organisations because it is much easier to understand business problems and to measure success through profit and loss. Even if bad management is masked because a firm stays in profit for a number of years due to intrinsically favourable market conditions, a badly run business will ultimately fold. Bad management in a public sector organisation will not manifest itself in the same way. Instead there is a lowering of performance in terms of both efficiency and effectiveness, morale decline, staff turnover often rises, sickness and absence may increase and recruitment may suffer. 'In many ways managing in organisations without clear financial parameters is much more difficult than managing in the business world. A public sector organisation is often very confused about what its outcomes are, and there is often an equal amount of confusion in the customers' minds about what constitutes a good product or service' (Harvey-Jones 1992: 154). A traditional argument thrown at public sector organisations and those that work in them is that they see their continuation as an end in itself; the bureaucracy of the public sector is as much a means of self-preservation as it is of ensuring impartial delivery of public service. The lack of clear focus is still a common problem. Many public sector organisations still have a major problem in developing the clear sense of mission exhorted by all writers and researchers on organisational success. Without this it is difficult to provide a firm foundation for the consciously developed set of coherent expectations supported by thoughtful performance management processes necessary to develop, maintain and communicate an appropriate model of managerial effectiveness.

'Non-profits fail to perform unless they start out with their mission. For the mission defines what results are in this particular non-profit institution' (Drucker 1990: 83). An example of this (Drucker 1992) is the CEO of a hospital chain who understood that she and her staff were in the business of delivering health care, not running hospitals. As a result of this reappraisal of their mission, movement of services out into the community was embraced rather than fought, with a consequent 15 per cent increase in revenue.

Drucker's aphorism about effectiveness discussed in Chapter 3, 'effectiveness is doing the right things right', means that the first step is to decide what the right things are. If, as is being suggested, defining and agreeing the right things in public sector organisations is more difficult than in many private sector organisations, then a model of managerial effectiveness that is based on supporting the achievements of the mission becomes difficult to articulate. Doing things well, i.e. efficiency, may provide a substitute framework for setting expectations and describing associated behaviour. This framework, however, is entirely about how things are to be done, with outcomes being separately related to specific tasks and objectives that may have no coherent organisational framework. This fragmented set of managerial activities could be described and rewarded as effective, depending on the particular standpoint or constituency of the observer.

Managing the cultural context in the public sector

The management of public services is clearly different from managing manufacturing and is also different from managing private sector services. In the private sector, the purpose or mission is to provide a service which is sufficiently attractive to potential customers to cause them to buy it. Public sector organisations have not traditionally had to generate income, though to a limited extent this has changed in recent years, with organisations like the DVLA selling for profit cherished number plates, and the internal market in the NHS generating a degree of real competition between trusts to provide better and cheaper services. However the choice available to the consumer of a public service is still very limited and will probably always be so unless there is an even more radical rethink of the nature and purpose of public services.

Flynn (1990) poses three fundamental questions in relation to culture, relevant to the current situation of the public sector:

1 is it possible to create organisations in which everyone shares the same values?
2 to deliver a responsive service, is it actually necessary that all employees share the same values?
3 is it possible to influence behaviour, even if values are not shared, by building on a particular type of organisation in which staff can work together?

He argues that attempting to develop shared values as a means of developing a commonality of means and ends is only possible 'if it is possible to create a congruence between what drives individuals and what organisations wish to achieve' (p. 151). If values are not shared then the structure of rewards, incentive and controls should be managed to encourage behaviour which manifests the organisation's values. The implication of this is that the organisation must enforce the compliance of the people in it by a variety of carrot-and-stick methods. Managers are the agents of that enforcement and effective managers would be those that achieved a given (minimum) degree of compliance.

Williams *et al.* (1993) define culture as 'the commonly held and relatively stable beliefs, attitudes and values that exist within the organisation' (p. 14). It is seen as something that clearly has an impact on organisational effectiveness. The beliefs held by managers and staff are the key influence on the nature of the organisation's culture and are both an input and output. Culture defines behaviour through the belief system. The definition above refers to 'commonly held' rather than 'shared' beliefs. In other words, the development of a particular set of beliefs – for example, about what constitutes managerial effectiveness – may be instinctive rather than deliberate. Miles and Snow (1978) found that the managerial culture influences the organisation's objectives, strategies and systems and that it is more important than environmental factors in guiding organisational response; unless and until external factors of such strengths are created that they forcibly challenge the existing managerial beliefs, resulting in adaptation or painful destruction and replacement.

Culture affects decision making, priorities and standards of performance and the norms and patterns of behaviour. In addition it can result in feelings of satisfaction and commitment or of alienation and dissatisfaction depending on the congruence between organisational demands and personal beliefs. If culture 'represents the collective conscious and unconscious of the organisation and that forms the basis for the interpretation of meaning, [it] is a pervasive influence on organisational behaviour and as such a significant determinant of organisational performance' (Williams *et al.* 1993: 37).

Beliefs held by individual managers reflect the culture and determine their behaviour. A belief can be described as the information that an individual possesses about something, usually some quality or characteristic, e.g. that X is an effective manager. Beliefs are learnt from observation or experience. Normally the receipt of supportive or contradictory information alters our belief, e.g. X did not receive performance-related pay this year therefore X is not an effective manager, and possibly 'therefore I should not behave like X'. Attitudes can generally be described as an effective response to a particular thing, idea or characteristic, something one likes or dislikes, whereas values tend to overlap with attitudes but have more of an evaluative or even moral dimension. Values involve agreement or disagreement. Attitudes, values and behaviours are all dependent on beliefs. Different sets of beliefs may underlie each one, though they will probably overlap considerably. Nevertheless we may find managers differing between what they would like and feel they ought to do and what the organisational environment, the expectations of significant others, dictates they do.

The way we behave is influenced mainly by our beliefs about various situational contingencies rather than our attitudes to events or people, e.g. beliefs about rewards versus costs associated with certain types of behaviour, the likelihood of success or failure, our own capability and our beliefs about the expectations of others. It is quite possible to have positive attitudes toward the organisation or our job but this alone will not result in managers behaving in a particular way. Sets of beliefs may differ and there will not always be a correlation between each set; so if an organisation wants its managers to adopt a particular form of behaviour, a change in attitude alone will not be sufficient, even if a manager develops a liking for or even agreement with a particular form of behaviour. It will be his or her beliefs about the rewards and costs associated with the particular form of behaviour that will decide whether or not they are practised. The probability of that behaviour having a successful work outcome, beliefs that the manager has about their capability to perform the required behaviour, perceptions by others in the organisation of the manager acting in a socially desirable way; all form part of the reward/cost belief system. Many of these beliefs that affect behaviour are gained from working in a particular organisation, even for a short time. Therefore the various systems and processes that affect behaviour may need to be changed and to be integrated – for example, reward systems, information and resources for particular tasks, the work processes and design of work, job training and development – to support the acquisition and understanding of particular skills and behaviours, etc.

To change the culture of the organisation, behaviour has to be changed by changing commonly held beliefs through managing the variables in the work environment that affect beliefs. Therefore any intervention to change culture can be assessed in terms of its value in this respect. Williams *et al.*'s (1993) study of various organisations concluded that major changes in an organisation's systems, e.g. reward, structure or technology may by themselves result in behavioural and cultural change. A change in behaviour can be enforced through teaching people new techniques and behaviours without addressing beliefs, attitudes or values directly. But failure to consider how people actually feel about doing something different or whether they agree with it can result in minimal compliance and even antagonism or subversion; it can be very stressful for the individuals in the organisation. Compliance can be demanded but there is often a price to pay in terms of overall effectiveness and efficiency. But congruence between attitudes, values and behaviour results in a strong and effective culture with high levels of personal commitment rather than enforced compliance.

Most of the organisations studied by Williams and others (a mix of eight UK private and public sector organisations) saw leadership at the top and throughout the organisation as a critical driver and shaper of culture change. The collection of behaviours adopted by managers (their 'style') acts as a role model and gives messages to staff. It reflects a combination of their personal values and their beliefs about the organisation and its environment.

Autocratic behaviour may be a reflection of the belief that given the situation – the nature of the task, time pressures, undertrained and overworked staff – it may be more effective rather than a reflection of an intrinsic theory 'X' attitude (i.e. that people dislike work and will only do it if directed and coerced) (McGregor 1960). Similarly insisting that managers adopt a participative style when the organisation is traditional, rule-bound and bureaucratic is unlikely to produce a congruency between manager and situation. Any manager attempting to fully embrace such a style in these circumstances is likely to be viewed as ineffective.

Schein (1985) considers that the behaviour of leaders at the top of the organisation is the major factor in cultural change. They act as role models for leaders of teams, groups and departments at different levels in the organisation. What is it that they pay attention to, what do they measure and control? How do they react to major organisational events and crises? What behaviours do they deliberately model, teach and coach? What criteria do they apply in rewarding managers and staff, and in selection, promotion and 'letting go'?

Given some of the real differences between public and private sector organisations there do seem to be limitations on the ability of leaders in public sector organisations to change beliefs because of the constraints of politics and public accountability in the public sector, irrespective of the fact that there has been some separation of management from the political process. It may therefore be the situation that change in public sector organisations is ultimately a reactive process led by external factors such as government policy and ideology. If this is the case, the public sector context may never be able to produce quite so clear a set of expectations or behaviours that constitute effective managerial performance as the best private sector organisations. This may simply be one of the differentiating factors between managing in the public sector in contrast to the private sector. The process of defining managerial effectiveness has to take account of a greater degree of ambiguity in the public sector. The definition may need to include certain behaviours and characteristics which encompass, in a positive way, the highly contingent and fluid nature of effective public sector management by placing a high premium on adaptability and a tolerance for ambiguity.

The difficulties experienced in operationalising the concept of effectiveness have been especially problematic for the human resource (HR) function as it often finds itself involved in a number of processes that implicitly rather than explicitly assume that there is a clear and agreed notion of managerial effectiveness. It is not appropriate in this text to examine the human resource function in great detail but one or two examples may be useful to illustrate the nature of the problem.

Effectiveness and the human resource function

The achievement of any change, improvement in service quality or performance outcome, however defined or measured in any organisation, is dependent on the people in that organisation. All successful organisations must acquire the capability to review continuously their operations and activities and then seek to improve upon any identified deficiencies. This rather simplistic statement of organisational behaviour perhaps masks the complexity and pressure that responding to continuous change imposes upon individuals within the organisation. The external environment in which an organisation exists can serve to add to and exacerbate these demands. The public sector environment has experienced a number of particular challenges of this nature: shifting political priorities, limitation on resources, a tendency to short-termism, piecemeal initiatives and internal markets. In order to cope with these forces, staff have had to continuously appraise, adjust and acquire new skills and approaches. This is of course not achieved without cost to the individual in terms of levels of stress, and to the organisation in terms of morale and performance. The issue of performance assessment is acutely affected by these processes since the behaviours associated with good performance are difficult to assess; indeed output measures themselves have become different and hence unstable. Some traditional HR approaches have found it difficult to adapt to this turbulent environment.

If we define the purpose of HR management as facilitating the achievement of business goals, then it follows that virtually all HR policies could have some impact upon the match between behaviours and goals. For example, if pay systems are altered without reference to organisational structures or the capability of staff, then they are likely to be ineffectual and possibly counterproductive. It is important that HR activities are integrated with each other and with the business. Workforce planning, often seen as the starting point for many HR processes, puts considerable emphasis upon the clarity of the links between business goals and skills needed in terms of creating competitive performance. The whole concept of shaping an organisation's workforce so as to improve overall organisational performance contains implicit assumptions about what behaviours are appropriate. In many instances workforce planning processes operate without this information and tend to make assumptions, along traditional and historic lines, that broad categories of skills will be adequate. It is not surprising then, that workforce planning is often regarded as too slow and unable to respond to the demands of a rapidly changing market.

It is almost self-evident that this issue of knowing which behaviours make a difference is equally vital to the provision of training and development for managers. There are of course a large number of developmental processes, ranging from formal courses aimed at the acquisition of knowledge and techniques to more action-learning events where, through direct experience, the participant is expected to assimilate relevant skills and processes. It is not appropriate here to discuss each of these in detail. More important is the recognition that all approaches are based upon the assumption that the resultant 'improved' manager will be better equipped to support organisational objectives. This assumption is of course vulnerable to the cynical cost-conscious line manager, who fails to see any obvious link between the training experience and performance back on the job. For management developers this same vulnerability is a challenge to demonstrate, in terms of value for money, that development programmes are of measurable benefit to the organisation.

Management competency

The rush to embrace the term 'competency' during the 1980s is in part a response to the same challenge. The term, despite its ambiguities (whether based on task- or person-orientated approaches) none the less appears to offer a way of bridging the gap between what managers do and how this affects the organisation. This rather idealised comprehensive solution spurred the growth of generic models of competency. However, increasingly the contextual and cultural factors within different organisations have come to the fore, with organisations such as BP and Cadbury Schweppes developing their own specific competency models. However, as Iles (1993) comments, it is interesting that these specific company-based models, which identify characteristics such as achievement orientation and situational flexibility, resemble some of the more generic models such as the competencies identified by Boyatzis (1982). The notion that competency can provide the appropriate link between behaviour and performance is reinforced by Iles in his suggestion that competency could provide a coherent framework for HR activities. He points out, though, that two conditions must be met:

- the competencies must have within them some concept of future development, thus avoiding becoming historic and dated
- there must be internal consistency so that the model is integral to all elements of HR activities.

He suggests that the idea of career management may offer a useful way of ensuring such integration.

Williams *et al.*'s (1993) study found that it was after the 'mundane tools' of personnel management were used in a coordinated and integrated way that the necessary changes in an organisation's culture were slowly and inexorably, over time, brought about. The processes of selection, induction, communication, training and development, appraisal and performance review, etc., if used tactically within an overall HR strategy that is based on the needs of the organisation, can all work together to instil and reinforce the beliefs and behaviours that the organisation has defined. It is the consistency and constant attention that will establish a desirable model of managerial effectiveness, once it has been properly articulated, shared and understood.

One particularly helpful notion of competence is offered by Boam and Sparrow (1992). They relate competencies to business life cycles and business environments so that a particular competency will have its own life cycle. Some competencies may be emerging and perhaps not be particularly relevant at present, but the changes in organisational direction may well make greater demand upon this competency in the future. Such a consideration would obviously make sense in terms of many public services with new commercial and entrepreneurial skills becoming increasingly relevant. Other competencies might be said to be maturing (becoming less relevant), others could be transitional between different environments, and yet others, such as analytic ability, might be said to be core competencies. Clearly the implication of this argument is that the relative importance of any one competence may vary according to the business environment or strategic path adopted by the organisation. The contingency model of performance as discussed earlier is entirely consistent with this concept of relative competencies. The relevant behaviours/competencies which affect performance will change; therefore in creating effective organisations it is important that this fluidity is understood and encompassed.

Reddin (1970), although emphasising the quantitative and measurable aspects of performance as an index of effectiveness, also makes it clear that 'effectiveness results from the appropriateness of a particular style of management to the demands of the situation in which it is applied' (p. 88). Thus although Reddin's philosophy is output-orientated and more allied to the concept of management by objectives, he still sees the need for managers to recognise the need and to adjust behaviours as required. Helping managers and organisations make explicit these needs is the crucial task.

Holmes and Joyce (1993) reinforce the strength of this position by emphasising that competency refers to 'the relationship between anticipated performance and performance required' (p. 41). Thus we are talking about anticipated or inferred behaviour and the degree to which it is in line with the performance needed by the organisation. If the process of defining competencies can incorporate both task-based requirements as well as role-based expectations, then competencies offer a dynamic framework for linking the behavioural repertoire of managers with organisational performance.

There is a third area which some approaches to competence would also include, that of personal characteristics of the individual manager. This aspect has typically become a focus for those seeing the key to management development as equivalent to the development of self (Mann and Pedler 1992). Although there is a considerable self-development competency literature, for the most part HR practitioners have tended to approach individual personal characteristics through selection processes.

Selection

Traditionally, personnel selection has taken a predominantly organisational or managerial perspective. As such, it aims to select the best person or persons for a job. 'Best' may have a number of implications, such as training time or retention but inevitably it will also imply an aspect of good performance. In this sense, selection has operated as an agent of the organisation and with a concern for organisational outcomes. More recently the dual interest nature of the selection process has been emphasised by Herriot (1989a). He describes selection as a two-way process involving mutual exploration, negotiation and agreement on expectations. Thus again we see the increasing influence of the contingency approach, whereby both individual and organisation must be in accord for effective performance to be attained.

There are many approaches to selection processes, such as interviews, psychometric tests, work samples and assessment centres. All have their merits and deficiencies and are very well reviewed by Herriot (1989b). Perhaps the common feature of all approaches to selection and of greatest relevance to our argument here is their need to establish criterion measures. None of the selection techniques can be validated unless we are clear what criteria we should be using to judge their predictive power. Criterion measures lie at the heart of selection and typically involve some form of performance measure. Unfortunately there are great difficulties in identifying agreed and stable criteria. The main problem is that it is rare for a single performance measure to be an adequate reflection of the multi-faceted nature of performance, especially in a situation such as management. Although techniques such as behavioural checklists and training can help, the 'criterion problem' remains a profound problem for selection. It is not possible to determine the success of a particular test or measure unless we can define and measure the behaviour associated with organisational success.

Once again we see a traditional HR technique bedevilled by the concept of effectiveness. Whether it is a lack of shared expectation at the point of recruitment or the absence of acceptable criterion measures, the subjective and variable nature of performance presents a severe obstacle to effective selection.

The majority of these difficulties come to a head in terms of appraisal processes and notions of performance-related pay. The latter is currently of particular interest to the public service, especially the health sector, where the government is keen to see performance-related pay introduced to all professional staff. Obviously there are many controversial aspects to this initiative, especially where the performance of doctors is concerned. Even with managerial staff, where such systems have been in place for some time, problems remain.

Appraisal and Individual Performance Review (IPR) systems have attracted considerable criticism as leading to overly bureaucratic recording systems which do not address the real issues or as making rather gross judgements about concepts such as loyalty of staff or effectiveness with little evidence. Johnson (1992) identifies some of the key factors that need to be in place for an appraisal system to work well. Two of the key aspects he suggests are a shared understanding so as to be clear about expected performance, and determining beforehand how performance in the various aspects of the job will be assessed.

It is clear that if traditional HR techniques are to operate successfully, the issue of performance or effectiveness must be integrated into all aspects of HR systems. Whether it is recruitment, selection, training and development or appraisal, they can only support the achievement of organisational goals if the concept of individual effectiveness is clear. The key mechanism from the HR repertoire is appraisal and this will be examined in the next chapter.

Appraisal and performance
review systems

This chapter examines a key management system by which the effectiveness of individual managers is assessed and developed. Performance appraisal systems – by whatever title they are referred to in different organisations, which may reflect different purposes or philosophies – have had a chequered history but have developed in sophistication over time. They are integral to the performance of organisations. Like any management system, if thought through and introduced into the organisation in an integrated way, they can be a fundamental tool for bringing about higher organisational performance and strategic and cultural shift through increasing the effectiveness of individual managers.

The development of the approach to
appraisal

There are a number of broad stages through which general thinking about appraisal has moved. As described earlier, organisations must develop a clear picture of the effective manager against which to appraise performance. Thinking about what constitutes effective performance has changed over the years. Early approaches focused on personality traits and attempted to assess the extent to which individuals displayed desirable characteristics. According to McGregor (1957: 89), 'the manager [should] pass judgement on the personal worth of subordinates'. Clearly some personality traits such as decisiveness are important in management, but in such schemes there is no sense of a relationship between such traits and the purpose, content or out-come of management jobs. McGregor's work on building the appraisal process around the achievement of work-related objectives helped to move thinking forward so that the process of appraisal became more job-specific with a clear emphasis on results. With hindsight it could be argued that the MBO approach developed by Drucker (1954) had two weaknesses. Firstly, 'this approach calls on the subordinate to establish short-term performance goals for himself', i.e. it encouraged a short-term view of performance (McGregor 1957). Secondly, although the 'superior's role is to help the man relate his self-appraisal, his "targets" and his plans for the ensuing period to the realities of the organisation', the relationship of individual work and effort to wider team and corporate goals did not, in practice, seem to be given great emphasis. This fault may have been more a result of unsophisticated management thinking on the implementation of the scheme, or a lesser degree of awareness at that time of the concept of corporate culture and strategy and the need for integration. However, these faults are equally apparent today.

With the inevitable time-lag that occurs before there is a real and fundamental change in actual management practice (as against super-ficial flirting with managerial fads and fashion) many organisations were still introducing new schemes of appraisal based on a very tradi-tional approach to MBO during the 1980s. The NHS scheme of indi-vidual performance review introduced in 1986 (DHSS 1986) referred to in Chapter 2 was, effectively, the first non-trait-related scheme for managers in this major public sector organisation. But it was and to a great extent still is in practice an entirely objectives-related system that does little to consciously develop a desirable set of behaviours based on a clear model of effectiveness.

There were, however, a number of organisations that during the late 1980s had already begun to move beyond this approach to perform-ance review schemes based on a combination of objective setting and the development of competencies – job-related behaviours that are particularly important in enabling individual managers to achieve their objectives which we discussed earlier. Usually these competencies are seen to be organisation-specific either in the language used and/or in their relative importance to a particular organisational context. Exam-ples of such competencies are those developed by Cadbury Schweppes (Glaze 1989) or Manchester Airport (Jackson 1989). These approaches have the virtue of not only setting out the task (objectives) of the manager but also indicating the process (appropriate behaviours and skills) that the organisation believes will help support the completion of the task in an organisationally appropriate way. They also, most importantly, show how individual managers can increase their individual effectiveness by developing relevant competencies. Competencies differ from personality traits in being observable behaviours. If a manager possesses such competencies, he or she can undertake management tasks and functions to a higher standard, i.e. competencies are job-related. The competency movement is still getting established and there is much developmental work being undertaken.

The current stage of thinking in the development of appraisal is to set it within the total context of managing performance in organisations. We have seen the emergence in recent years of performance management as an identifiable management idea; though one not yet fully defined in absolute terms (IPM 1992). Although the research undertaken by the Institute of Personnel Management demonstrates a diversity of management systems of constituting what organisations refer to as 'performance management' one overall characteristic appears to be an attempt to integrate the management of all systems and process that affect organisational performance, with some form of individual appraisal system as the core. It can be said that the 'MBO plus competencies' type of approach may over-emphasise these two components and in doing so overlook the interrelationship of other factors in the organisation that affect individual performance. In practice the development of competencies as an idea has only preceded the emergence of the performance management idea by a few years, and so not all organisations have yet got to grips with competencies. The advantages of the performance management approach is that at its best it places appraisal in a holistic framework of interacting processes, all of which need to be managed in order to provide a meaningful and worthwhile context for the individual appraisal of managers, which is at the heart of performance management. Such an approach must bring organisations, and the managers running them, to a point where the question 'what constitutes effective performance in our organisation?' is addressed, which in turn must lead on to the question 'what is it that managers have to do to achieve that performance?' – how can they be effective?

If there is a next phase in the development of thinking about appraisal then it is probably in the coming together of the concept of the learning organisation with that of performance management. Such an approach may encompass the management of all organisational systems so that they not only perform well in the current organisational situation but also maintain future performance by anticipating and preparing for the coming situation and making this a constant process. Appraisal then becomes a tool for increasing managerial effectiveness through facilitating managerial learning and developing the capacity to learn how to learn, at both an individual and a corporate level. The latter is dependent on the former.

So performance appraisal has developed from what now appears to be a rather simplistic assessment of certain desirable personality traits to being part of a sophisticated and possibly rather complicated process for managing performance and of assessing and developing the capacity for managerial learning. It aims at maintaining and increasing effectiveness next year and the year after and the years to come. It has moved from a unidimensional to a multidimensional approach.

Over the same period a number of other trends in development are discernible. A shift from a closed judgmental process conducted by others to an open (though still in most cases confidential) process based on self-appraisal and, in some cases, multiple appraisal involving peers, subordinates and senior managers other than 'the boss'. The setting of objectives and performance targets has also generally moved toward a self-generated rather than other-generated or imposed process. Within the context of a performance management approach we also see increasing emphasis on the 'job' of the team or group within which a manager must operate, as well as that of the individual manager, in recognition of the interaction and cooperation that is required to achieve many of the more complex tasks in organisations.

The issue of judgemental versus developmental approaches, the associated questions of motivation, reward and performance-related pay, and the degree to which systems encourage a prospective or retrospective approach are also crucial to the success of appraisal schemes in increasing the effectiveness of individual managers.

The purpose of appraisal

Any organisation that introduces a system designed to improve performance must be clear about the purpose of that system. What do we want from it, what approach is required to achieve what we want and how will it fit with other systems that will both affect it and be affected by it?

In the context of our discussion in this book, the critical outcome required from an appraisal scheme is a reinforcement of a common, organisationally appropriate model of individual managerial effectiveness. Different organisations may quite legitimately end up with different models against which appraisal takes place. There is clearly no one generic model that fits all managerial jobs in all organisations. Each organisation needs to evolve its own definition or profile of the effective manager which pulls together outcomes required, i.e. performance objectives and targets, and the set of behaviours and skills that will fit the culture and context of that organisation. There is merit in each organisation reinventing the wheel if this means there takes place an involving process that describes and sets out the organisation's model of effectiveness in an understandable form.

It is critical that this work is done prior to the implementation of appraisal in order to provide the necessary framework. The increasingly sophisticated approach to competency development provides a means of doing this, but many organisations fail to lay this foundation. Many organisations go straight to the design of the appraisal system, and even then there may be unclear thinking about the purpose of the scheme.

Organisations can pile so many objectives on to an appraisal system that it fails to meet most or all of them. For example:

- to review past performance
- to decide on performance-related pay
- to set performance objectives for next year – in a team and/or organisational context, as appropriate
- to identify development needs and opportunities
- to redefine the purpose and role of the job in response to continuing organisational change
- to discuss future personal and career development.

A system intended to do all of the above is almost bound to fail. Firstly, because there is seemingly too much work to do within the scheme, and the amount of time required is considerable, especially if appraisal still tends to be the non-integrated once-a-year event. Secondly, some of the objectives for the scheme are possibly in conflict with each other. For example, setting performance-related pay requires a retrospective look and may inhibit any open discussion of development needs in case this is perceived as indicative of poor performance and reduces pay levels. Going back over the previous year may provide a good foundation for the performance requirements of the following year, but it can be a wasteful process if it prevents sufficient time being spent on looking forward to new and changing requirements. As organisations and priorities change it will be important to spend time redefining the purpose of the job, its role within and its relationship to the organisation before focusing on specific objectives and targets. In any event, objectives set at one point in time can exceed their sell-by date as events move on, so frequent review and updating is required. If the emphasis is on judging performance then there may be little emphasis given to discussing personal and career development. This may either directly affect individual performance, especially if new ways of working to achieve objectives are required and they are not fully discussed. Or it may demotivate because personal aspirations are not being given any importance by the organisation. Consequently key managers may leave at a bad time for the organisation.

So it is important to disentangle the different purposes for which schemes may be run, and then to ensure that the design of the system matches the stated purpose. It may ultimately be better to have separate schemes, e.g. one for performance review and pay and another for personal and career development.

The term 'appraisal' seems to be used far less than in the past. The various titles given to the schemes seem to suggest the particular purpose of a scheme. However, titles can be misleading, sometimes reflecting vague intentions rather than reality. For example, a career development scheme may in practice tend to ignore personal aspirations and career moves and be devoted to objectives and target setting for the present job, and review achievement on a retrospective basis. Sometimes schemes are designed with a particular intention which is reflected in the title, e.g. performance review, but because of prevailing cultural norms or the lack of an overriding corporate culture, they may be hijacked by individuals themselves to accommodate personal needs and aspirations at the expense of the organisation's needs.

Though it is not always explicitly stated, most schemes are performance-orientated, particularly at managerial level because they use objective and target setting approaches. Whether this problem is then tackled primarily on a judgemental retrospective basis or a developmental-prospective basis is dependent on the culture and values of the organisation.

Any scheme, by whatever title, cannot aid managerial effectiveness if it is in itself ineffective. As discussed earlier, effectiveness will be a subjective concept unless it is related to an agreed and understood purpose. The setting up of a scheme must involve debate and clarification of its purpose, how that purpose is to be achieved and what inputs (for example, system design, involvement of those who have to generate it, appropriate training, sufficient time) are required for the purpose to be achieved in the manner required. The scheme or system is a means to the end of increasing individual effectiveness; individual effectiveness is a means to the end of increasing organisational effectiveness and success. Any management scheme or system must contribute something. It cannot be allowed to be an end in itself or it will cease to have meaning in the organisational context and be seen as a burden by those that have to operate it, with all the obvious consequences of wasted and unproductive effort.

Problems with conducting appraisal

Any system of appraisal can suffer from a number of operational problems stemming from inadequate design or implementation.

Appraisal can be a disconnected activity where the scheme seems to stick out like a sore thumb unconnected to any other organisational activity. It can have no link to the corporate business planning process, to pay and reward strategies and systems, or training and development strategies. If an organisation is consciously adopting a performance management approach and/or embracing an integrated approach to human resource management then, by definition, this ought not to happen. There is a high probability that the operation of an appraisal scheme in this way is indicative of all the management process in the organisation generally being a dis-integrated collection of systems and activities. The development of an organisationally appropriate model of effectiveness derived from a rigorous and involving process among the managers of the organisation is fundamental to getting it right.

The annual event was mentioned earlier where everything that needs to be done is done at one or at best two sessions, at a particular point each year with little or no discussion on the objectives set or other issues raised at any other time. Performance is a continuous effect and requires managing continuously. It can go up or down for a variety of reasons. For example, individuals may continue to work on 'objectives ousted by other priorities' (the OOOPs phenomenon). They may not receive previously agreed development or training, such as coaching or guided experience from their manager or off-the-job skill instruction, which was intended to help them achieve required performance levels. They may become demotivated because personal aspirations and career issues seem not to matter and have received no further attention. If too much is expected of a scheme, then a once-a-year event cannot encompass everything in any depth.

Individual effectiveness may be dependent to a greater or lesser degree on the overall effectiveness of particular groups or teams in which the individual participates. If this is not recognised, then the scheme may be so individually orientated that it could cause conflict within the groups or teams crucial to organisational success. An obvious example is where performance-related pay is linked to individual performance through the appraisal scheme and takes no account of the need for, or results of, cooperative group effort, thereby apparently encouraging managers to put individual interests first. Even if pay is not part of the equation, unproductive dynamics can be created if the scheme does not place both the clarification of job purpose and role and the setting and achievement of objectives within the context of a group or team. Some jobs and some objectives may be almost entirely dependent on cooperative effort, though some may be much more individualistic.

Because some form of face-to-face interview or discussion is critical to the conduct of effective appraisal, the interpersonal skills required, particularly of the appraiser, are of a high order. It is not unusual to find managers approaching the appraisal of their subordinates with fear and trepidation, even where they feel positive about the individual to be appraised. Sitting down with another person, being expected to initiate and guide a discussion about how that person carries out their job, and then giving useful feedback is something that many people find inhibiting. Even giving feedback that is based on praise for good performance can be difficult. Making it specific enough for the individual concerned to be able to replicate it or build on it requires prior thought and information about the way the appraisee has worked at meeting their objectives and consideration of how to communicate this to the appraisee. Guiding the discussion towards self-appraisal requires even more thought, preparation and consideration of the existing rapport and trust. It also demands attention to an approach based more on questioning than making statements about the person's work and performance (Rackham and Morgan 1977).

The problems for the appraiser may be compounded by the fact that the appraisee, whilst possibly apprehensive, often has very high expectations of their 'time with the boss', especially if it is their first appraisal. If the starting point is a situation where there is existing ill-feeling or mistrust, this has to be dealt with first. Of course it may not be. The introduction of an appraisal process into the organisation will not solely solve these problems. It provides an opportunity to do so but it may end up making them worse. But with the right sort of guidance and training and the right approach by the manager (i.e. adequate preparation), many of the perceived difficulties can be reduced. Appraisal based on feedback is a practical skill which requires practice. The once-a-year event, or the confining of such discussion to the formal procedure, does not give appraising managers sufficient practice to develop these skills as part of their normal repertoire and to build the associated confidence that comes with frequent use.

If the approach to a scheme is too informal, a coffee-table chat that gives little feedback and sticks to generalities, the appraisee is left none the wiser. However, many schemes suffer from the opposite problem of over-formalised, complex, highly structured systems often with a depressing weight of paperwork. It is important to find the right balance. The organisation must signal the importance of the process and it must fit the culture and expectations of the managers in the organisation. Too much structure and paperwork can mean that managers get lost amongst the proverbial trees, chopping down as many as they can to manufacture the mountain of paper they need for the forms they have to fill in! The scheme becomes an end in itself that gets in the way of effective performance. The supporting system must facilitate the appraisal or review of performance or development needs, or whatever the agreed purpose of the scheme is, with minimum effort. It must be sufficient to give guidance and to ensure that the important things happen. However, as managers become more experienced they need less structured support.

Although we keep referring to the 'scheme' or 'system', appraisal is more of a philosophy of managing others. It may require a system to support it, particularly early on. But if the principles on which the philosophy is based are clearly understood, the model of effectiveness it is trying to build is clear to all, and the outcomes required from the scheme clearly defined, then in ideal circumstances the system need have no formal paperwork at all. If managers apply the principles and achieve the outcomes in terms of increased effectiveness, then appraisal (and all that is implied by this term) has become *the* way of managing instead of a new trick or bolt-on extra.

The aim of introducing an appraisal scheme, or renovating an existing one, should be to make it so much part of the fabric of the organisation, an intrinsic part of the culture, that any new manager joining the organisation absorbs the underlying principles through the osmotic process of socialisation that affects anyone joining a new organisation. At the same time, there should be a firm message conveyed about 'getting it right', through mandatory training backing up a clear statement of purpose, principles and outcomes.

One of the reasons for appraisal schemes failing (and indeed other systems designed to improve performance), is that the period of development and implementation is too short. British organisations, both public and private sector, are frequently accused of short-termism. Short-term thinking, whether in commercial investment strategies or in the planning of public services beyond the yearly budget cycle, is the norm. With management schemes and process that require the development and acceptance of new beliefs and behaviours, organisations are either too impatient for a pay-off or lack the stamina for the sustained effort necessary to fully integrate and bed-in a new philosophy and supporting systems. Organisations that seem to have got it more right than others talk in terms of three to four years of constant coordinated effort to develop their approach to appraisal. They also say that it needs to be part of an integrated strategy designed to promulgate the organisation's model of effectiveness.

Being too judgemental is another fairly common problem which inhibits open discussion on actual performance and can lead to a manipulative approach when attempting to set or agree performance targets. The appraisee may see the process as a threat and want to give themselves maximum room for manoeuvre by having the targets as loose and low level as possible. The appraiser may attempt to impose targets which are unachievable or to which the appraisee has no real commitment. The appraisee may not have the skills or resources to achieve objectives or to match expectations about effective managerial behaviour but does not feel able to bring this into the discussion.

If this is the predominant experience of appraisees in an organisation, then it is probable that it is simply a manifestation of the prevailing culture. Some managers and some organisations value 'macho' behaviour. 'Get it done and take no prisoners!' Sometimes these values are explicitly stated; often they are hidden behind espoused values and statements about developing, nurturing and caring. In the former case, particularly in more extreme cases, it is probable that an air of threat and fear pervades management activity. It may produce short-term high performance whilst existing environmental factors remain constant, but it will not encourage questioning, risk-taking and the experimentation and creativity required to both identify and deal with changing environmental factors. The potential for individual and organisational learning that might be facilitated by appraisal systems is negated.

Where an organisational espouses one set of values but manifests another through its actions and activities, additional factors of confusion, frustration and cynicism enter the equation. What beliefs will the manager hold? The policy papers supporting the introduction of the scheme may set out the objectives of personal and career development as a means of increasing motivation and practical ability in order to generate higher organisational performance; the supporting training may, at least in the full flush of initial resourcing, appear to support these principles; however, the practice and the experience of those being appraised is different. The hoped-for personal or career development processes or opportunities do not appear or are only short-lived; the emphasis is on judging success at achieving performance targets. Within a relatively short period of time the briefly enthused staff realise that normal service has been resumed. The effect on overall performance is likely to be downward and the organisation might have been better off spending any money and resources expended on the scheme on something else.

In spite of all the virtues of an objectives-based appraisal or performance review scheme in terms of decreasing subjectivity and amateur personality assessment, there is an inherent danger of over-emphasising results or ends at the expense of means. Achieving objectives or targets *per se* is not always a demonstration of managerial effectiveness. Managers must be equally concerned with the quality of the process by which objectives and targets are achieved. The means can be as important as the ends. An obvious example is the swift blitzkrieg approach to cost-cutting or the introduction of new technology. Cost targets may be on schedule for end-of-year figures but the cuts may be strategically damaging or cause so much resentment that guerrilla warfare breaks out among managers and departments, who are fighting for individual survival rather than corporate gain or customer (or patient or client) services. A new computer system installed too quickly could easily result in inadequate testing and comparison of systems against need and their operation in the particular organisational environment. Or there could have been insufficient attention to checking the level of skills and training required to operate the new systems, in relation to existing skills or the lead time and cost of training staff. Hindsight may illustrate that the quality of the process used by a manager has in fact meant that an objective apparently achieved has come apart and that the longer-term affect of achievement is ineffective performance in terms of the overall health of the organisation.

Paying for performance

One of the more recent examinations of the issue of whether pay is a major contribution to higher performance is the research organised by the Institute of Personnel Management referred to earlier. The first part of the study was conducted by Bevan and Thompson during 1991, and published in 1992. It was followed up by Fletcher and Williams during 1991 and 1992, and published in 1992. Both stages of the study question the reliance that many employers place on pay as a means of motivating high performance.

Where pay is just one part of a reward strategy that takes into account what employees actually perceive as 'reward' (i.e. what is important to them rather than what employers assume is important), it has more chance of contributing to higher performance. They also found evidence that a pay-based reward-driven approach to performance management which takes little or no account of personal, job and career development needs is likely to be less successful than one that does.

What works is the integrated approach where PRP is only one element in a holistic performance management strategy incorporating both reward (as against simply pay) and development. 'PRP appears to work best after the issues of training and development have been addressed' (IPM 1992: 138). Training and development are often perceived as part of reward and as motivators in their own right, particularly if there is a link with personal development and career progression.

The inhibiting effect of pay-related judgements on open and honest discussion about performance referred to earlier is also identified by the research. Additionally, the amount of PRP offered, the degree of flexibility in mixing pay and other rewards, and the immediacy and directness of the link between effort and reward were all factors influencing the effectiveness of PRP. Where the operation of PRP was influenced by the need to limit wages because of financial constraints or cash limits, as in the case of public sector organisations, this produced a much more cynical response. In general, the research found a very simplistic approach to PRP in spite of the fact that 74 per cent of the organisations studied by Bevan and Thompson had some form of PRP system. For managers, appraisal-related PRP was by far the most common approach, as against profit sharing, merit pay without an appraisal, individual bonuses, team bonuses or share options.

However, changes in organisational structures and the nature and design of work are prompting greater attention to rewarding team rather than individual performance. Many organisations that had worked with some form of PRP for a number of years were considering moving on to approaches that reflected team and overall organisational performance. One of the case studies cited by Fletcher and Williams, a pharmaceutical company that seemed to have got it more right than most, set out to ensure that individuals understood and were committed to the objectives and performance targets of the work group, which provided the basis for their own job clarification process and for setting their own individual targets. In training managers in the operation of the scheme, the need for balance between individual and team needs and objectives was highlighted. When PRP was assessed, it was the subject of a shared debate between managers. The 'boss' made a recommendation which was shared with both other senior managers and with peers.

Bevan and Thompson also found that 68 per cent of organisations separated discussions about pay and performance. Fletcher and Williams found that in some of the case study organisations they examined there was a very direct link between appraisal and pay, with the latter being determined by the former, though often with some time gap between the two activities. At the other end of the spectrum were a range of organisations where PRP was entirely separate from appraisal.

Throughout the research there was no consistency of view on the power of money alone to motivate higher performance. In fact it was clear that if mishandled PRP would decrease motivation.

Developing and implementing an appraisal scheme

Figure 6.1 attempts to provide a framework for the issues and activities that have to be addressed in designing or overhauling an appraisal system. In terms of the purpose of the scheme, as we discussed earlier, it must help to reduce the subjectivity of views about individual managerial effectiveness and establish a clear profile against which to judge performance that incorporates organisationally relevant performance targets which are achieved through the employment of organisationally appropriate behaviours and skills. In line with the ideas of performance management, appraisal cannot stand alone as a system for managing performance. If individual managers are to be effective in their contribution to organisational performance, an integrated strategy of supporting activities and policies must be developed and followed. This immediately moves the traditional personnel department task of paperwork design and setting up supporting workshops to a much later stage in the process than they traditionally came. The work implied by the framework should not be seen as a reason for putting off appraisal until next year; it is an indication of the fundamental need to address all these issues on a continuing basis in order to ensure organisational survival and success.

Where to start? Logically one would start with the clarification of corporate goals and requirements derived from a widespread and thorough debate about organisational purpose, a sharing of a sense of future mission and the development of a widely discussed and accepted mission statement. To do that effectively requires confident leadership that embodies an appropriate balance between transformational and transactional elements (Flanagan and Thompson 1993), organisational values that assume the importance of individuals in the organisation being a party to that process both in their own right and in organisationally relevant teams, plus effective systems of communication

Figure 6.1 A framework for managing individual performance and effectiveness

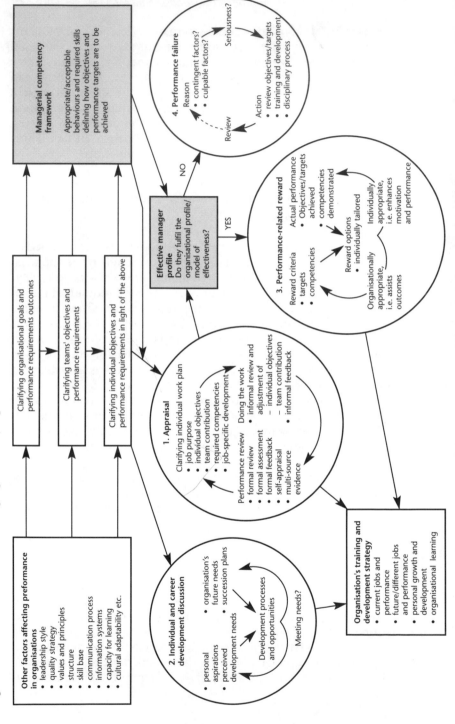

that facilitate the transfer of information and meaning and the involvement of the workforce.

In terms of the model one would then move on to the 'team(s) performance requirements' (whether whole business units, departments or specific project or task teams) and then to the individual manager's performance requirements. This provides the foundation for the supporting systems and processes (1 to 4) to do with managing the performance, development and reward of individual managers.

In practice, many of these areas are tackled in parallel. The process is interactive; some areas are accomplished relatively easily and some not. Large elements may already be in place, such as a mature training and development strategy which may only need to reorientate the focus of its activities. Those responsible for driving the whole process may need to take an opportunistic approach, seizing some opportunity such as competitive threat, new products emerging, government changes, profit or budget allocation increases, poor performance, feedback from staff or managers through an attitude survey indicating dissatisfaction, the loss of some key staff or managers to competitors, etc.

One important lesson from the IPM research is to ensure that the whole process is line management owned and driven from the start, with assistance, facilitation and advice – but not sole ownership – from the human resource specialists. Line managers must be involved fully in the development of the 'effective manager profile' for their organisation, the systems for appraising against this model, the supporting developmental process, and the implementation and review of the whole process, over time, in terms of its value to the organisation.

All of the managerial activities require guidance and backup training for managers in how to do them. Managers at all levels need to feel both confident and competent in carrying out these activities and to understand their purpose and interrelationship. The operation of the various systems and processes supporting the management of performance become in themselves objectives and targets for managers. The manner of their achievement is governed by the relevant behaviours and applied skills embodied in the 'managerial competency framework'.

A constant theme throughout this book is the development of an organisation-specific effectiveness/competency model. This is critical and various techniques such as the repertory grid can be used to get under the superficial descriptions often used to define effective or well-performing managers. This is demonstrated by the research discussed in Chapter 8. The technique can be used to construct an agreed and common model of effectiveness on the well-performing manager and a common language for describing what it is this individual actually does and should do in a particular organisation. One possible danger is that if this model is entirely internally derived, without both the awareness of the need for testing its relevance and the application of a rigorous method for doing this, it could end up as simply a calcified clarification of the *status quo*. The avoidance of 'groupthink' and the inherent complacency or lack of challenge associated with it must be avoided (Janis 1973). The emerging model must be interrogated in terms of both its current relevance to effective performance and its capacity to provide a basis for a future and, if necessary, a different model of effectiveness.

Having established an organisationally relevant model and developed a common language for interpreting it, managers have a model against which to assess their own and their colleagues' performance and to discuss development needs. There is then a much stronger foundation for the whole appraisal and development processes.

There does, however, remain the issue of categorisation referred to in Chapter 4 and the collecting of first-hand evidence of how a manager undertakes his or her job. The biases inherent in categorisation should be minimised by the development of an organisational model, provided its development really does involve all managers in the organisation and its promulgation and maintenance are reinforced through regular discussion, sharing and interrogation. The need for this should not be viewed as 'something to do with training' or outside the real business of management. It should be understood to be fundamental to the constant need for strategic reappraisal of organisational performance. 'What is it that we as managers are trying to achieve and how are we going about it?' The appraisal process should help provide more objective answers to these questions by reinforcing the need for evidence of what managers actually do, rather than assumptions about what we think they do. Making available evidence of actual work performance as a basis for appraisal may require a rethink of the traditional boss–subordinate appraisal. Greater use of self, peer, subordinate and other senior manager appraisals will help to produce real knowledge about what a particular manager actually does. So too, will different approaches within the face-to-face interview – 'What have you actually done in relation to this objective or target; how did you go about doing it?' Making the philosophy and principles of appraisal part of the culture rather than 'a system' is the key to the process. As Williams *et al.* (1993: 144) say: 'The appraisal system is another of the organisation's cultural artifacts and, like the payment system, its form and content sends out clear cultural messages.'

A practical examination of individual effectiveness

We have seen earlier that managerial effectiveness is a negotiable concept formed around interacting sets of expectations. Managers can create models of the reality of their organisational life which helps them understand what is going on. The models of the organisation held by managers may not all be the same but it is probable that there will be some overlap. The degree of overlap will be dependent on the extent to which models are shared, discussed and evaluated. The sharing process, even when positively attempted, may run into difficulties over the variability in the language different people use to describe their views. Management has no agreed language, therefore when concepts are expressed at an individual level semantic choice in expression adds to the sense of confusion as to what each person means by something like 'effectiveness'.

Theoretical statements about effectiveness would then appear to have inherent limitations since they must opt for one linguistic structure or another, thus potentially excluding or running counter to the model held by others. It is within individuals and within organisations that an operational definition of effectiveness will emerge. In attempting to research the concept of effectiveness within the framework described here, i.e. individual expectations within a specific context, one must come to terms with the nature of the likely outcome. A final defining statement of what is effectiveness will probably remain elusive but a greater understanding of how people form and use their own concept of effectiveness should be achievable. It was with this latter prospect in mind that we undertook an empirical examination of individual effectiveness.

The theoretical framework for the investigation is based on Chapter 4. Thus a research programme examining effectiveness should take into account the following three points:

1 there is no agreed absolute definition of managerial effectiveness against which to test data, therefore any definition must be relative to and emerge from a given situation or context
2 it is the manager's own view of what effectiveness is, or might be, that is ultimately most influential in terms of the way he or she behaves
3 the method of research, of collecting the data, should impose no bias or preconceived framework on a participant's own perception of effectiveness.

If we are to find out how individual managers think about their work and their jobs, a method of study is necessary that enables managers to articulate their own individual perceptions and then uses those perceptions as the building blocks for developing a picture or description of effectiveness – to try and understand the constructs that particular individuals use to think about their jobs (Stewart 1989b). Langford (1979), in reviewing the various methods and approaches used in a wide range of studies of effectiveness, concluded that the repertory grid appears to be one of the most promising methods found so far. Grid interviews, though requiring mastery of a particular technique and potentially very time-consuming, have the virtue of avoiding preconceptions, and minimise any bias on the part of the interviewer. They are designed to elicit the constructs that individuals use when thinking about the issue or person that forms the subject of the interview. Grid interviews yield more information than conventional interviews. One disadvantage is that because grids produce a unique individual picture, there is limited scope for comparison across grids unless either the constructs or the elements are constant. This may not always be appropriate in research that is trying to find out what managers in an organisation collectively think about effectiveness, contrasted with testing a particular view of effectiveness. However, grid information from a representative cross-section of the population to be surveyed can be used to produce a performance questionnaire which is much quicker to complete on an individual basis than grid interviews. It can therefore be used more easily and quickly with a larger number of people.

To understand why a manager behaves in a particular way – whether judged effective or ineffective – we need to know what has caused that behaviour. Have they made a conscious decision to undertake their job – to behave – in a particular way in relation to cues they perceive in the organisation, is it an unconscious reaction to such cues, or is it random behaviour? We therefore need to ask managers why they behaved in a particular way.

Gathering the data

The repertory grid process was used in a fairly standard form (Easterby-Smith 1980) in such a way that respondents were asked to identify three general managers known to them who they would describe as effective, three who they would say were ineffective, and three who they would regard as in between the two groups. They were then asked to 'look at three managers (drawn from the three subgroups) and think about them in terms of what makes them effective or ineffective in relation to the way they actually do their job. Is there any way in which two of them are similar but different to the third?' The managers were then rotated so that a series of comparisons can be made in the triadic structure. This continued until participants were unable to produce new constructs in describing the managers.

The data were gathered from five health authorities varying in locations (urban/rural) and in size of population served. Twenty participants in all took part in the data-gathering process, including health authority chairmen and women, district and unit general managers.

The repertory grid process produced 476 constructs in all describing perceptions of effectiveness. These were sorted into a set of overall categories (see Table 7.1).

There are many questions and forms of analysis that could be conducted using this data. For example, we have argued earlier that each organisation may well have a particular culture in terms of expectations of performance. This can be assessed by taking the responses from the participants in two different districts (see Table 7.2).

There are some clear differences implied in Table 7.2 about how senior managers in these two organisations think about effectiveness. The weighting in District B to category 8 'drive and commitment' could well indicate a more dynamic culture, where an energetic and possibly aggressive style of management is preferred. The reverse picture in category 7 and in category 3 may well indicate District A's more people-centred style of management. At an anecdotal level the potential cultural difference implied here was reflected in a strong sense of task orientation and business orientation in District B. Thus our first insight is that organisations differ in how they view effectiveness and this may well have implications for what sort of behaviours are expected from managers in these organisations. There would appear to be a strong contextual input to defining effectiveness.

Table 7.1 Effectiveness categories

	1	2	3	4	5	6	7	8
Label	Methods of approach to work	Nature and quality of working relationships	Management of subordinates	Clarity of vision	Background and experience	Temperament	Confidence and assurance	Drive and commitment
Content	Managerial, technical and professional skills and competencies, etc.	Autocratic/ democratic; interpersonal and political skills; persuasiveness; empathy; attitude to people; rapport	Loyalty; delegation; handling problems of subordinates; guidance; instruction; team building	Clear objectives; clarity of view and direction; long-term vision; strategic/ short-term important/ unimportant; alternatives and options; clear thinking and objectivity; clear analysis and definition of issues; measuring performance	Broad/narrow; qualifications; line/functional; administrative/ professional	Approachable; optimistic; pessimistic; anxiety; adaptability; resilience; complainer; evenness; use of humour; introvert/ extrovert	Natural authority inspires confidence, presence; firm courage; views; timidity	Challenging; outgoing; gets things done; staying power; energy; high profile; diffidence; laziness; high performer/ achiever; long hours of work

Comment	This category covers those aspects of the way a manager does his/her job which are not directly people-centred. Some of them might be viewed as a practical *outcome* of a particular view or philosophy or of certain personal qualities or preferences	This category covers those aspects of the way a manager does his or her job which are a direct product of a particular philosophy, set of values or attitudes toward other people and the skills associated with ability to handle other people	This category is closely related to 2 but covers those constructs which relate specifically to subordinates	This category is very much about bringing clarity out of confusion, setting clear and credible goals and direction and monitoring progress and performance	This category includes a range of inherent personal qualities and characteristics mainly to do with emotional toughness and stability	This category covers a range of constructs clustered around the concepts of self-confidence and charisma which might also be categorised under leadership and are to do with whether other people see the manager as someone they and others will follow or accept a lead from	This category centres on the concepts of energy and go-getting and of driving oneself, the team and the organisation along

Most of these categories have a degree of overlap because the various behaviours and characteristics described are not fully discrete. They may be linked in cause–effect terms or represent similar, but not the same, factors. They have been grouped on the basis of their clustering around one of eight main descriptions of aspects of effectiveness.

Table 7.2 District comparison

| | | Effectiveness categories | | | | | | | |
		1	2	3	4	5	6	7	8
District	A	19.8	17.5	15.0	11.0	3.0	3.0	15.5	8.7
District	B	16.8	18.0	11.3	8.4	6.7	6.3	10.5	16.8
Difference		3.0	0.5	3.7	2.6	3.7	8.3	5.0	8.1

The organisational differences may well contain considerable individual variation. The model of effectiveness described earlier suggests this may be an individual phenomenon influenced by both other individuals and the organisation. A comparison of some individual participants' views of effectiveness serves to underline this variation. For example, if we examine the two concepts 'delegation' and 'leadership', we find that elaboration of the two concepts reveals quite different levels of meaning as to quite what people mean by them.

'Delegation'

- 'delegates routine work'
- 'delegates real responsibility to subordinates'
- 'delegates large areas of work without appreciating what their orders involve'
- 'happy for other people to deal directly with their subordinates'
- 'develops subordinates through delegation'.

'Leadership'

- 'being seen to and known to have sympathy with people'
- 'a concern for people in the organisation'
- 'having a presence'
- 'being charismatic'
- 'eliciting the confidence of others'
- 'decisiveness'
- 'commitment to the NHS'
- 'courage'
- 'extroversion'.

Thus it is clear if two individuals were involved in appraising a subordinate's leadership potential they might well use the same language but would probably mean different behaviours.

More evidence of individual differences in the perception of effectiveness can be seen in a further analysis which used the ratings participants had made of the most important elements of effectiveness. A few examples drawn from just three participants serves to illustrate the variability and range of descriptive concepts used.

Top-rated effectiveness criteria

Subject 1

1 'meets targets, i.e. high output'
2 'uses and manipulates the system to achieve goals'
3 'action-orientated, gets things done'
4 'extremely committed and hard-working'.

Subject 2

1 'able to present a wider and balanced view of the service – can see things from outsider's viewpoint'
2 'has political awareness'
3 'has an ambassadorial approach'
4 'presents as a more experienced, balanced manager'.

Subject 3

1 'leads through example rather than authority'
2 'doesn't worry about things'
3 'sets a good example to subordinates'
4 'good at handling complex and long-term issues'.

It is self-evident that the concepts representing different individuals' key constructs about effectiveness reflect differences in what people feel to be important. Of course these are not directly statements about how these individuals behave in their work. This example does tell us, however, that subordinates who are judged against these criteria, but do not share the same perception of effectiveness, may not produce the behaviours that elicit a favourable assessment. A lack of congruence in terms of an individual's behaviour and the expectations of another person could be damaging to his or her future career prospects. It is clear though that someone deemed to be underperforming in this way may simply not have assimilated the relevant views and operations about what is seen as effective behaviour, rather than underperformed in any objective manner.

The information discussed so far tends to support the contention that effectiveness is a subjective concept. However, it must also be recognised that judgements of effectiveness often need to be taken for good practical reasons, such as appraisal and performance-related pay decisions. It would therefore be of considerable practical value if one could define a rather more universal concept of effectiveness.

In order to pursue this goal a questionnaire version for the repertory grid was developed. This resulted from a factor analysis of the initial constructs and was built around the items perceived to be the most important aspects of effectiveness. A total of 88 items were identified to constitute the managerial effectiveness questionnaire (see Appendix). It was decided to focus the questionnaire upon a particular job group, namely unit general managers. This group was chosen as being the critical point of operational management in the NHS and most generalisable to other parts of the public sector. In all, 78 managers were asked to complete the questionnaire about both the most effective and the least effective manager known to them. These respondents were drawn from 30 different health authorities, with ultimately 18 districts agreeing to participate.

The aim of the questionnaire was to provide a wider and more representative picture of effectiveness. The analysis initially produced three separate descriptive outcomes:

- a list of items that best distinguish between the effective and the ineffective manager
- a list of items associated with effectiveness
- a list of items associated with ineffectiveness.

The items constituting these actions are presented in Tables 7.3 and 7.4.

Our research activities seem, to us at least, to have succeeded and failed at the same time. The results from the repertory grid serve to support our fundamental proposition that managerial effectiveness has no agreed definition but varies between individuals. However, in classifying the 476 constructs into eight general categories, we have been guilty of ascribing common meaning with little external validity. The questionnaire has given us a useful tool for assessing broad views about effectiveness, but it has been developed within a particular context (a range of health authorities) and there must be a question mark as to how well the items will transfer to other organisations.

In conclusion we can say that individual managers:

- have different perceptions of the elements of effective/ineffective managerial behaviour

Table 7.3 Behaviour which best distinguishes effective from ineffective managers

Items which are most closely or closely associated with effectiveness *and* which differentiate strongly or very strongly between effectiveness and ineffectiveness (41 in total fulfilled these criteria)

Q. no.	Association with effectiveness (rank)		Very strong/ strong differentiator
84	5	Treats medical staff as equals	very strong
45	6	Clear thinker	very strong
81	8	Adapts readily to changing circumstances	strong
54	10	Tries to set a personal example to subordinates	very strong
59	11	Will take and enforce unpopular decisions when required	very strong
43	12	Prepared to take risks if he/ she thinks it will get things moving	very strong
61	12	Is resilient and recovers quickly from setbacks	very strong
49	14	Has a very cheerful disposition injecting humour even in the most serious situation	very strong
27	15	Initiates a lot of contacts with medical staff	strong
78	15	Meets targets and deadlines without being chased	strong
39	17	His/her self-confidence rubs off on others	strong
20	18	Likes to be creative and put forward new ideas	strong
58	18	Others tend to defer to his/her proposals and decisions	strong
2	20	Is generous in giving credit to others	very strong
21	21	Has a wide network of contacts	strong
29	22	Seeks to draw people together to develop ideas and get action	very strong
46	22	Is able to define and set objectives clearly	strong
60	25	Works energetically and quickly	strong

Table 7.3 Cont'd

Q. no.	Association with effectiveness (rank)		Very strong/ strong differentiator
38	26	Uses the delegation of tasks, responsibility and authority to stretch and develop subordinates	strong
51	28	Is happy for other managers to deal directly with subordinates	strong
50	29	Pays a lot of attention to the development of his/her team, e.g. through the selection and development of individual managers and time out events	very strong
34	30	Displays a strong loyalty toward subordinates	strong
3	32	In relation to change puts a lot of effort into ensuring that people understand not only *what* has to be done but *why*	strong
40	33	Gives responsibility and authority to subordinates to take decisions on important matters	very strong
1	35	Appears to be able to take criticism	very strong
87	38	Happier managing people rather than systems or strategies	very strong
32	41	Displays insight into the concerns and worries of other people	strong
82	42	Is never openly critical of subordinates	strong
15	44	Prefers to communicate face to face	strong
80	45	Behaves in a predictable and consistent way	very strong
8	46	Is quite prepared to be unpopular with subordinates in order to achieve targets	very strong
22	46	Tries to ensure that people feel comfortable in his/her company	very strong
46	47	Is able to define and set objectives clearly	strong

Table 7.3 Cont'd

Q. no.	Association with effectiveness (rank)		Very strong/ strong differentiator
16	49	Actually seeks to promote his/her unit on a District or supra-District basis.	very strong
76	49	Provides and considers a number of clear options for dealing with issues	very strong
86	51	Has moved around a lot in his/ her career, e.g. different jobs in the NHS and outside	very strong
74	54	Thinks through problems analytically	strong
13	56	Is very easy to get to know	strong
33	59	Has had formal management training	very strong
17	61	Is understanding of the sensitivities and attitudes of professional staff	strong
79	61	Views situations and issues dispassionately	strong

Note: The rank score indicates the position of this item in terms of its overall ranked association with effectiveness.

- vary in degree and kind in terms of their perception of the elements, though there are common elements
- vary in the complexity of their perceptions about effectiveness
- vary in the clarity of their perceptions about effectiveness
- vary in their ability to articulate these perceptions
- ascribe different meanings to the words they use to describe their perceptions.

Given this picture, organisations need to be careful about assuming a shared and common view of effectiveness. Instead they need to ask what might have conditioned a particular perception. Are there specific critical events? Is it a general impression? Is it from direct interpersonal contact? These questions may be difficult to answer, and indeed it must be recognised that some managers are more 'situationally sensitive' than others and thus capable of successfully reading very subtle indirect cues. It is important that apparent poor performance

Table 7.4 Behaviours most associated with ineffectiveness

Items which are most closely or closely associated with ineffectiveness *and* which very strongly or strongly differentiate between effectiveness and ineffectiveness (25 in total were found to meet these criteria)

Q. no.	Association with effectiveness (rank)		Very strong/ strong differentiator
39	1	Generates feelings of uncertainty in others	strong
78	2	Tends to slow up if difficulties accumulate and needs to be prompted	very strong
87	3	Happier managing systems and strategies rather than people	strong
76	5	Sometimes has difficulty in identifying alternative options for action	very strong
40	6	Wants subordinates to check with him/her before any substantial decisions are made, i.e. does not delegate responsibility and authority on important matters	very strong
15	8	Generates a lot of written communication	strong
1	10	Reacts badly to criticism	very strong
50	11	Gives little specific attention to the development of his/her team	very strong
70	11	Likes to mix with people of like mind, i.e. avoids people who have different views and perceptions	strong
32	10	Does not display any great insight into the concerns and worries of other people	strong
58	21	Others tend to question his/her proposals and decisions	strong
54	22	Tends more to 'do as I say' rather than 'do as I do', i.e. doesn't try to set a personal example to subordinates	very strong
79	23	Tends to be emotionally involved in decisions	strong
13	24	Takes time to get to know	strong

Table 7.4 Cont'd

Q. no.	Association with effectiveness (rank)		Very strong/ strong differentiator
21	25	Has a selective network of contacts, i.e. does not have a wide network	strong
81	25	Finds it difficult to adapt to changing circumstances	strong
43	28	Will take risks only if there is no alternative	very strong
46	28	Is (still) learning how to define and set objectives clearly	strong
47	30	Tends to be more pragmatic, i.e. does not have a strategic vision which guides actions and decisions	strong
62	30	Prefers to work alone	strong
82	32	Can be openly critical of subordinates	strong
20	33	Needs a good reason to change the *status quo*	strong
22	33	Is not particularly concerned whether people feel comfortable in his/her company	very strong
28	35	Believes the job has to be done even if staff are adversely affected, i.e. doesn't adapt approach to take account of the effect on people	strong
34	36	Tends to accept criticisms of subordinates from other managers and act accordingly	strong

be analysed in terms of possible lack of congruence in expectations. Finally, if the organisation discovers the existence of widespread incongruence it needs to decide what it does to create more appropriate expectations to sustain organisational achievement. The approaches outlined in this chapter will undoubtedly help an organisation create a stronger shared view of its performance expectations – perhaps a critical component of becoming a successful organisation.

| Chapter | **A summary for action** |
| eight | **and the future** |

This chapter tries to summarise some of the key action points arising out of the preceding seven chapters and discusses some of the issues which will provide the future context for managerial effectiveness.

An action summary

There is no single clear picture of effective management or effective managers. It is situationally dependent and varies from one organisation to another and within one organisation over time. The variations may be large or small but we believe that it is the variable element that can make the difference between being effective or not. The first key skill is the ability to read one's situation in a way that is both analytical and intuitive and to recognise that intuition is a cognitive skill which can be developed. Reading one's situation requires a sensitivity to the many factors which combine around a manager; this can be crudely summarised in terms of the interaction between an individual person and a specific job in a particular organisation.

Managers need to understand the highly subjective nature of judgements or descriptions of effectiveness and the need to capture and compare those held by individuals. Differences in descriptions of the various components of effectiveness are not just semantics, but probably represent important differences in assumptions, beliefs and perspectives about what constitutes effective managerial behaviour. Each person has their own mental model of effectiveness. If differences are not first clarified and then tested to understand their impact on performance through the individual behaviour of managers and their decisions in selecting, appraising and developing other managers and staff, then at best there will be an incoherent set of expectations within the organisation or at worst a set of expectations which damage the overall performance of the organisation by encouraging, albeit not deliberately, ineffective behaviour.

There seems to be an increasing body of opinion that performance effectiveness in not-for-profit and public sector organisations is based on a confused view of the purpose of the organisation, what it should be concentrating its resources on, and what measurement of performance it should use.

The complex range of organisational goals, some which may be in contradiction, produce a confused background of messages for individual managers in the organisation about what to do and how to do it. There are competing sets of expectations which the individual must balance and negotiate.

Left at this, some individuals will develop the skills of reading these expectations and be able to influence or renegotiate them, or will possess an appropriate set of other skills which allow them to enact them. Some will do it consciously, others reactively. This may simply result in a reputational effectiveness that contributes little to organisational performance. The combined effect of expectations and resultant behaviour can be described as the culture of the organisation, in other words, the way it is, or what it feels like to be in it.

The culture can be managed or changed, given time, to one that is more appropriate, through the integrated management of various management tools and systems, particularly those that affect people and their beliefs about what is important to the organisation. What the appropriate culture *is* for the organisation (that is, its people) depends on them developing a clear, shared and common view of the purpose of the organisation and its priorities. The organisation must also decide how these are to be achieved. The key group in this process are the managers in the organisation, including the top managers.

The single, most important message is not to assume that there is a commonly understood model of managerial effectiveness but that it is critically important to make the prevailing model explicit and then to interrogate its value to the organisation. A checklist of key points for action is given below which provides the basis of a long-term strategy. As always, the key responsibility falls on top managers, who need to act to make sure the following seven issues are addressed:

1 to have a common and agreed view among managers and other key constituents about:

(a) the organisation's purpose and priorities

(b) the principles which will guide how these are to be achieved

2 to examine all systems and processes to decide:

(a) whether they support achievement of the purpose and priorities

(b) whether they currently operate on the basis of the guiding principles

3 to help managers to develop or improve their skills at reading their situations. This requires:

(a) both analytical skills and a willingness to develop what we currently refer to as intuition, as a way of handling the more complex situations we find in organisations which exceed the ability of rational thought processes to deal with them

(b) to expand their capacity to learn through learning how to learn

4 to be prepared to use methods such as repertory grids as a means of defining and articulating:

(a) the current models of effectiveness individual managers hold and to which they currently work

(b) the cumulative effect of these models in terms of a management culture

5 to develop an understanding of how they make decisions on selecting assessment/appraisal, development needs, etc.:

(a) how this is affected by their mental model of effective behaviour

(b) the cumulative effect on the performance of individuals and of the organisation of these decisions

6 to understand the increasingly critical need for the development of a learning culture in organisations:

(a) based on a model of managerial effectiveness that embraces the ability to learn

(b) accepts genuine mistakes as a basis for real learning and development

7 to implement good performance management processes based on the centrality of an appropriate approach to appraisal/performance review which:

(a) promulgates the desired model of managerial effectiveness and develops situational and other skills based on the model

(b) becomes a way of managing rather than a labour-intensive system.

The future context

What of future models of managerial effectiveness in public sector organisations? There are three basic issues:

1 the distinctive nature of public sector management in relation to private sector management
2 the changing environment, national and international, for all organisations and the consequences for the nature of the management job, e.g. ambiguity being a norm
3 development in thinking and research about the nature of effective management skills or competencies, e.g. cognition, emotional/mental adaptability and how to help managers acquire these skills, e.g. learning how to learn and the learning organisation.

Integral to many of the reforms in public sector during the last 15 years is a view of management and its place in the public sector. 'Management' has pushed out 'administration'. The former stems from the private sector and is seen to be tougher and more performance-orientated than administration, which was more to do with maintaining services in a *status quo* situation. An increasingly challengeable assumption is that the same managers and management process can deliver the goods equally well in public or private sector organisations. Flynn (1990) describes managerial values as being in conflict with those professions that provide services to users, who see themselves as largely independent of management. He puts the managerial–professional tension against that of being inward-looking or outward-looking to produce four possible culture types:

1 where managers dominate and the culture is inward-looking, they produce an obsession with budgets and procedures and ignore the user
2 where the professionals dominate an inward-looking culture, they set their own standards irrespective of the needs of the community they serve
3 where professionals do try to take account of community needs
4 where managers control but are outward-looking toward customers and strive to make the whole organisation culturally responsive.

The recent wave of reforms are largely based on this latter assumption.

But, as Flynn points out 'what if that effort produces greater expectations and more demand for the service' (p. 180). The total budget is fixed, irrespective of competitive processes, so rationing takes place, based on both political and professional judgements about entitlement and needs. Such judgements and the processes associated with them are very different to private sector marketing decisions and there is no selling process linking customer and company. This 'means that the wholesale importation of private sector management techniques and the ideologies that go with them is inappropriate' (p. 181).

'The public sector accountability structures make managers' jobs different from those of managers of private services' (p. 184). The public sector has an ambiguous accountability which 'has no parallel in the private sector, where managers are ultimately accountable to shareholders' (Day and Klein 1987: 184). This ambiguity means that public sector managers must devote a lot of energy to managing the interface between their organisation and the political process. It is unavoidable and creates a degree of complexity in defining managerial roles, responsibilities and activities not usually found in private sector organisations, where other pressures may replace the diffuse and ambiguous nature of the management task.

Handy (1989) and Peters (1992) and others describe new highly fluid, post-hierarchical organisations in both the private and the public sector. There are many public sector examples of the 'shamrock principle' (workforce divided into core, contracted-out and part-time/temporary workers) in action with increasing numbers of portfolio workers who undertake a variety of paid and unpaid work for different clients providing services. In the NHS the idea is being discussed of the NHS trust as a 'holding company', managing the interrelationships between a whole range of independent and semi-independent agencies through a carefully defined contracting process as a means of providing health care services.

Kotter and Heskett (1992) describe the 'adaptive culture' or Theory 111 cultures. 'Only cultures that can help organisations anticipate and adapt to environmental change will be associated with superior performance over long periods of time' (p. 44). Although they are talking mainly about private sector organisations there are a number of characteristics which are particularly relevant to the public sector. It is a particular type of adaptive culture, one that meets the interests of all the constituencies that support an organisation, that is important when thinking about public sector organisations with multiple stockholders.

> Only when managers care about the legitimate interests of stockholders do they strive to perform well economically over time, and in a competitive industry that is only possible when they take care of their customers, and in a competitive labour market, that is only possible when they take care of those who serve the customers – employees'.
>
> (p. 46)

The parallel with the various constituencies of public sector organisations is easy to see. In less adaptive cultures managers behave more cautiously and politically to protect or advance themselves, their product or service and immediate work groups. Much of the criticism of public sector organisations reflects these latter characteristics.

The adaptive approach is underpinned by 'fairness to everyone . . . an emphasis on "integrity" of "doing the right thing"' (p. 52). Public sector organisations were traditionally characterised as benign and paternalistic in their attitude to the people who worked in them. Many managers now describe their organisation's cultures and the wider environment of that organisation as threatening (Flanagan and Henry 1993; Thompson *et al.* 1994). Much of the sense of threat may come from the stress of constantly having to adapt and change, often without much constructive support or help, but there seems to be a sense that integrity has given way to expediency.

In terms of managing the culture, what seems to differentiate the high from the low performers is 'in the case of the better performers, the leaders got their managers to buy into a timeless philosophy or set of values that stressed both meeting constituency needs and leadership or some other engine for change – values that cynics would liken to motherhood, but that when followed can be very powerful . . . they worked at it' (Kotter and Heskett 1992: 55). Given the sense of service to the public that ought to prevail in public sector organisations, this characteristic should be innate in the public sector. But there are as many cynics and self-interest groups as one might expect to find in the worst caricature of private sector organisations. These cynics are found equally among the leaders of both management and professions. The recent reforms may be used by some as a reason for an increase in cynicism because of the fundamental principles which they believe are under attack. There is an equal measure of cynicism generated by the loss of control and influence among some groups. Although there are limitations on the extent to which even top managers in public sector organisations can be leaders because of public and political accountability, they need to keep working on their managers and professional heads to develop and keep reviewing their coherent vision of the service. This makes it easier to see many changes as changes in means rather than ends.

Top managers studied by Kotter and Heskett helped perpetuate adaptive values by talking about them and writing about them, by behaving in ways consistent with those values, by hiring and promoting people whose own values were consistent with core values (but did not demand blind conformity), and by ensuring that organisational systems and processes reinforced adaptive values. 'They were usually quick to spot a proposed compensation system or performance appraisal process that would not reflect the core philosophy of the firm'

(Kotter and Heskett 1992: 56). This is the same point made by Williams *et al.* (1993) when they discuss the need to ensure that all the basic management systems and processes support the development and maintenance of the type of culture required. Selection of the right people in the first place was often easier than trying to change them once they were inside the organisation. People with the right qualities should be selected to match the model of effectiveness needed by the organisation. It is these ordinary management tools, the artefacts of the organisation's culture, that make the real difference in the long run rather than the large-scale heroic intervention that is usually a single episode in the life of the organisation.

Morgan (1988) identifies nine competencies for 'riding the waves of change'. He talks about the need to develop outside-in management where managers relate to the external environment in terms of what is necessary to meet the challenge of new technologies and the evolving demands of external stakeholders, especially customers and potential customers rather than considering the environment from the perspective of what we, in this organisation, would like to do. The approach is based upon mentally standing outside one's own organisation and roving around the external environment looking at the relevant technology, market-place, strengths and weaknesses of one's own organisation in order to anticipate the transformations required and the key competencies that need developing and strengthening.

According to Agor (1985: 5):

> Top managers often find that left brain analytical techniques (for example, management by objectives, PERT and forecasting) are not always as useful as they once were for guiding decisions. This is so because top executives now have to make major decisions in a climate characterised by rapid change and at times also laden with crisis events. In addition, emerging new trends often make linear models based on past trends either inaccurate or misleading.
>
> (p. 6)

A sample of top executives showed that they 'strongly believed that intuition was one of the skills they used to guide their most important decisions' (p. 16). The 'research suggests that the effective use of intuition could well be a significant factor in increasing managerial productivity in the decade ahead' (p. 17). Agor puts forward a number of reasons:

- research into how the brain functions is growing
- processes such as intuition are better understood, as are methods for enhancing them

- it is becoming a more acceptable management skill (especially among top managers) – though a majority will still attempt to cover up
- opportunities exist for honing and developing the skill.

Kolb *et al.* (1986: 20) state that 'From the perspective of management development we see increasingly that the organisation's ability to survive and thrive in a complex dynamic environment is constrained by the capabilities of managers who must learn to manage both the greater environmental complexity and the complex organisational forms developed to cope with the environment.' They emphasise the need for learning and criticise much management development for producing in managers a general pattern of limited vision and a lack of knowledge. This results from a systematic failure to provide managers with opportunities to learn and to prepare for the complex realities they face. 'The complex organisational structures and management systems required to deal effectively with environmental complexity and change are not working; primarily because managers are not prepared to use them effectively' (p. 21). For example, though much in vogue, matrix management confuses because much more is required of managers than in classical organisation structure. The level of overall competence required of managers is generally much higher. Kolb and his colleagues discuss four areas of competence which are all required to be effective in the face of more complex demands:

> Greater *behavioral* competence in taking initiative and responsibility under conditions of risk and uncertainty, greater *perceptual* competence in gathering and organising information and taking the perspective of different organisational sub-units, greater *affective* competence in empathising with others and in resolving conflicts among managers with different viewpoints and greater *symbolic* competence in one's ability to conceptualise the organisation as a system, are all required to make modern organisational forms work effectively.
>
> (p. 22)

Management development programmes must be linked to the strategic mission of the organisation and that mission must be clear and must be worked on so that it provides a framework within which to locate the model of effectiveness the programme is designed to support.

Management development requirements must be based on an analysis of strategic projections for the organisation's future environment. Educational programmes then have to be developed to help managers prepare in advance for these more complex responsibilities. There is a fundamental need 'to identify not only highly specialised, specific knowledge requirements, but also the more integrative learning and problem solving competencies needed to cope with uncertainty and complexity' (p. 23).

> Experiential learning is a basis for developing a two-dimensional 'competency circle' which arranges the special adaptive competencies of managerial knowledge around the experiential learning cycle – affective competencies/concrete experience; perceptual/ reflective observation; symbolic/abstract conceptualisation; behavioral/active experimentation.
>
> (p. 23)

This focus on adaptive learning competence accomplishes two things. Firstly, if we accept that adaptation and learning are the central characteristics of all person/situation transactions then the competency circle technique is holistic, making it possible to compare and contrast the essential learning needs in different jobs, in different organisations, career paths and professions. Secondly, the focus on competence emphasises the importance of congruence or 'fit' between managerial knowledge and job demands. Competence is not a judgement about an individual alone, but about the effective match, or congruity, between individual knowledge and skill and work environment demands: in other words, the manager's situation. The competency circle approach defines individual knowledge and job demands in commensurate terms so that this effective match can be determined. 'Mismatches between current and future job demands and current managerial knowledge identify the educational objectives for management development programmes' (p. 20).

Senge (1992: 176) states that 'As the basic learning disciplines start to become assimilated into an organisation, a different view of managerial work will develop. Action will still be critical, but *incisive action will not be confused with incessant activity*. There will be time for reflection, conceptualising and examining complex issues.' It is not possible to specify how much time managers in future organisations will spend reflecting, modelling and designing learning processes but it is hoped that it will be a great deal more than is currently the case.

Great ideas and brilliant strategies fail not just from, or evenly mainly from, motivational weakness or even non-systemic understanding, but from limited mental models of the world. More specifically, new insights fail to get put into practice because they conflict with deeply held internal images of how the world works, images that limit us to familiar ways of thinking and acting. That is why a managed process of articulating individual and collective mental models – surfacing, testing and improving the individual and collective picture of how the world works – could be a major breakthrough in building effective organisations with effective managers who learn through articulating, interrogating and adapting their internal pictures. Managers' mental models are often systematically flawed. They are not based on the sensitivity to their situation that results in learning and adaptation of behaviour, including seeking out new skills and knowledge relevant to the needs and demands of their work environment. Managerial effectiveness is a largely subjective concept specific to a situation and must be defined in the context of that situation. Most, if not all organisation situations, whether public or private, are in a constant state of flux making the ability to learn and adapt accordingly fundamental to becoming and remaining an effective manager in future organisations.

Performance management is an inherent part of the public sector culture. Organisations which are good at performance management focus on the effectiveness of managers, particularly their senior managers. Only greater clarity about what constitutes effective managerial behaviour and management of the factors which affect it through selection, assessment and development will lead to better organisational performance.

Appendix	***Management effectiveness –***
	unit general managers:
	performance questionnaire

PLEASE READ CAREFULLY THE FOLLOWING *BEFORE* YOU COMPLETE THE QUESTIONNAIRE

As you will know from my earlier letter I am undertaking a research study into the characteristics of effectiveness in relation to Unit General Managers. I understand that you have agreed to participate in the study by completing two questionnaires. The first one is attached.

Please note that your responses will be kept completely confidential and that their will be no attribution to individuals participating in the study.

In order for the questionnaire to be completed in a useful way you are asked to have in mind *a real person who is a unit general manager* when completing it. For this first questionnaire you are asked to think of *the least effective unit general manager you know or have known* and to complete the questionnaire about him or her.

It is important to the research that we end up with a description of a real person, good points as well as bad. We do *not*, however, want to know this person's name or who they are.

Every item in the questionnaire consists of a pair of statements with a line between them. For each item decide which statement best describes the person you have in mind and put an 'x' at the appropriate point *on the line*, i.e. do you think the person you have in mind is nearer to the left hand description or the right hand description?

For example,

1 Is better at handling
   subordinates

Is better at handling
superiors

├────────────────────────×──────────────────────────┤

This would mean that you think he or she is usually better at handling subordinates but not always.

2   Would rather achieve targets

Would rather handle
organisational matters

├───────────────────────────────────────✕───┤

This would mean that you think he or she nearly always prefers to handle organisational issues and pays little attention to targets.

If you believe neither applies put N/A. If they are equally balanced between the two, place the 'x' in the middle of the line.

When you have completed the questionnaire please return it in the prepaid label provided to:

Hugh Flanagan, Health Services Management Centre, University of Birmingham

---

NAME: _____

MANAGERIAL EFFECTIVENESS – PERFORMANCE QUESTIONNAIRE

1   Appears to be able to take criticism

Reacts badly to criticism

├──┤

2   Is generous in giving credit to
others

Is slow to recognise the
achievements and contributions
of others

├──┤

3   In relation to change, puts a lot of
effort into ensuring that people
understand not only *what* has to
be done but *why*

Believes people have to adapt and
change even if they don't fully
understand or accept *why*

├──┤

4   Is not easily intimidated by other
managers and professional staff
who disagree with him/her

Can be intimidated by other
managers and professional staff

├──┤

5   Attempts to clarify priorities and
tasks for subordinates

Lets subordinates sort out their
own priorities and tasks

├──┤

6 Likes to take action quickly

Prefers to reflect before taking
action

|⊢—————————————————————————————⊣|

7 Has general managerial/
administrative background

Has a professional or technical
background

|⊢—————————————————————————————⊣|

8 Can allow desire to remain on
good terms with subordinates to
interfere with achieving targets

Is quite prepared to be unpopular
with subordinates in order to
achieve targets

|⊢—————————————————————————————⊣|

9 Has a detailed personal
understanding of the service
for which he/she is
responsible

Uses professional and technical
staff to provide a detailed
understanding of the service for
which he/she is responsible

|⊢—————————————————————————————⊣|

10 Is good at handling complex
long-term issues

Is good at handling immediate
crises

|⊢—————————————————————————————⊣|

11 Believes it is important to be
involved in routine work

Delegates all routine work to
subordinates

|⊢—————————————————————————————⊣|

12 Gives a lot of attention to
consumer (patient) needs

Gives a lot of attention to cost
improvements and efficiency
measures

|⊢—————————————————————————————⊣|

13 Is very easy to get to know

Takes time to get to know

|⊢—————————————————————————————⊣|

14 Takes a broad corporate view
of the organisation

Takes a very positive view of the
needs of their own unit

|⊢—————————————————————————————⊣|

15 Generates a lot of written
communication

Prefers to communicate face to
face

|⊢—————————————————————————————⊣|

16 Actively seeks to promote his/her
unit on a district or supra-
district basis

Devotes their time and energy to
the internal issues of the unit

|⊢—————————————————————————————⊣|

17 Is understanding of the sensitivities and attitudes of professional staff

Can be impatient of the sensitivities and attitudes of professional staff

├───┤

18 Likes situations where he/she has to think on their feet in presenting a case

Likes situations where they have to present carefully reasoned and documented evidence

├───┤

19 Is very organised and structured in the way he/she works

Is intuitive and spontaneous in the way he/she works

├───┤

20 Likes to be creative and put forward new ideas

Needs a good reason to change the *status quo*

├───┤

21 Has a wide network of contacts

Has a selective network of contacts

├───┤

22 Tries to ensure that people feel comfortable in their company

Is less concerned whether people feel comfortable in their company

├───┤

23 Demonstrates sound technical knowledge and ability in managing systems and procedures, e.g. personnel, finance and planning

Uses others' tachnical knowledge and ability in managing systems and procedures

├───┤

24 Takes account of political sensitivities when writing reports or papers

Believes in being as objective as possible when writing reports and papers

├───┤

25 Believes it is most important to ensure that work gets completed on time and to the required standard

Believes it is most important to give people confidence and help them to enjoy their work

├───┤

26 Is sensitive to public perceptions of issues and handles them accordingly

Handles public issues as he or she personally thinks is right

├───┤

27 Initiates a lot of contacts with   Lets contacts with medical staff
    medical staff   arise

    ├───┤

28 Thinks hard about the effect of   Believes the job has to be done
    decisions on people and alters   even if staff are adversely
    approach accordingly   affected

    ├───┤

29 Seeks to draw people together to   Prefers to let people go their own
    develop ideas and get action   way and initiate their own ideas
                                              and action

    ├───┤

30 Allows subordinates to take risks   Discourages any risk-taking on
    and to fail   the part of subordinates

    ├───┤

31 Spends a lot of time meeting   Spends a lot of time with people
    with people in their own   collectively in formal meetings
    departments or offices on a one-
    to-one basis

    ├───┤

32 Displays insight into the concerns   Does not display any great insight
    and worries of other people   into the concerns and worries of
                                              other people

    ├───┤

33 Has had formal management   Has had little or no formal
    training   management training

    ├───┤

34 Displays a strong loyalty towards   Tends to accept criticisms from
    subordinates   other managers of subordinates
                                              and acts accordingly

    ├───┤

35 Is well qualified academically, e.g.   Has minimum level of academic
    degree +   qualifications, e.g. O levels

    ├───┤

36 Follows the rules   Ignores the rules

    ├───┤

37 Has a 'machiavellian' approach   Has an open, consensus approach
    to getting things done   to getting things done

    ├───┤

38 Uses the delegation of tasks, responsibility and authority to stretch and develop subordinates

Pays no specific attention to the development needs of subordinates when delegating work

├───┤

39 His/her self-confidence rubs off on others

Generates feelings or uncertainty in others

├───────────────────────────   ───────────┤

40 Gives responsibility and authority to subordinates to take decisions on important matters

Wants subordinates to check with him/her before any substantial decisions are made

├───┤

41 Actively encourages a team approach with subordinates

Leads subordinates from the front

├────────   ──────────────────────────────┤

42 Has a consistent set of priorities and objectives

Is particularly sensitive to changing circumstances and alters objectives and priorities accordingly

├──────────────────────   ────────────────┤

43 Prepared to take risks if he/she thinks it will get things moving

Will take risks only if there is no alternative

├────────────   ──────────────────────────┤

44 Takes a wide view of an issue before taking action

Homes in on an issue and takes action quickly

├───┤

45 Clear thinker

Disorganised thinker

├──────────   ────────────────────────────┤

46 Is able to define and set objectives clearly

Is learning how to define and set objectives clearly

├───┤

47 Has a strategic vision which guides actions and decisions

Tends to be more pragmatic

├─────────────────────────────   ─────────┤

48 Acts and speaks with confidence

Tends to be more reserved and deferential

├─────────   ───────────   ───────┤

49 Has a very cheerful disposition, injecting humour even in the most serious situation

Has a more phlegmatic and taciturn disposition

├──────────────────────────────────────┤

50 Pays a lot of attention to the development of their team, e.g. through the selection, and development of individual managers and time out events

Gives little specific attention to the development of their team

├──────────────────────────────────────┤

51 If happy for other senior managers to deal directly with subordinates

Discourages direct contact between senior managers and subordinates

├──────────────────────────────────────┤

52 Always willing to express an opinion or take a decision and and stand by it

More considered in putting forward an opinion or taking a decision and willing to modify it

├──────────────────────────────────────┤

53 Has a very high opinion of him-/herself

Tends to be self-deprecating

├──────────────────────────────────────┤

54 Tries to set a personal example to subordinates

Tends more to 'do as I say' than 'do as I do'

├──────────────────────────────────────┤

55 Has a strong, extrovert personality

Has a quieter, more polished personality

├──────────────────────────────────────┤

56 Adopts a very meticulous approach to detailed work

Becomes impatient when required to undertake detailed work

├──────────────────────────────────────┤

57 Has integrity

Is more pragmatic

├──────────────────────────────────────┤

58 Others tend to defer to his/her proposals and decisions

Others tend to question his/her proposals and decisions

├──────────────────────────────────────┤

59 Will take and enforce unpopular decisions when required

Needs a very good reason to take and enforce unpopular decisions

├──────────────────────────────┤

60 Works energetically and quickly

Is more measured and deliberate

├──────────────────────────────┤

61 Is resilient and recovers quickly from setbacks

Less resilient and may take longer to bounce back from setbacks

├──────────────────────────────┤

62 Prefers to work alone

Prefers to work with others

├──────────────────────────────┤

63 Is very competitive

Is more relaxed

├──────────────────────────────┤

64 Generally affable and even-tempered

Makes it clear to others when angry or upset

├──────────────────────────────┤

65 Works long hours on a regular basis

Works long hours on occasions

├──────────────────────────────┤

66 Uses words rather than statistics and numbers as a basis for argument, e.g. in presenting reports

Uses statistics and numbers rather than words as a basis for argument

├──────────────────────────────┤

67 Hardly ever shows anxiety or distress under pressure

Sometimes shows anxiety or distress under pressure

├──────────────────────────────┤

68 Tends to take centre stage

Lets others take centre stage

├──────────────────────────────┤

69 Is very aggressive and outspoken

Is more passive and reticent

├──────────────────────────────┤

70 Likes to mix with people who have different views and perceptions

Likes to mix with people of like mind

├──────────────────────────────┤

71 Go out of their way to be helpful

Don't put any great effort into being helpful

├──────────────────────────────┤

72 Is careful in forming judgements   Tends to form opinions of other
    of other people   people quickly

    ├───┤

73 Is very committed to the NHS   Is less strongly committed to the
                                              NHS

    ├───┤

74 Thinks through problems   Acts more on impulse and feel
    analytically

    ├───┤

75 Delegates but is very careful   Delegates and leaves
    to monitor progress   responsibilities with subordinates

    ├───┤

76 Provides and considers a number   Sometimes has difficulty in
    of clear options for dealing   identifying alternative options
    with issues   for action

    ├───┤

77 Finds talking to people very   Finds it difficult to talk to other
    easy   people

    ├───┤

78 Meets targets and deadlines   Tends to slow up if difficulties
    without being chased   accumulate and needs to be
                                              prompted

    ├───┤

79 Views situations and issues   Tends to be 'emotionally
    dispassionately   involved' in decisions

    ├───┤

80 Behaves in a predictable and   Behaviour can be unpredictable
    and consistent way   and inconsistent

    ├───┤

81 Adapts readily to changing   Finds it difficult to adapt to
    circumstances   changing circumstances

    ├───┤

82 Is never openly critical of   Can be openly critical of
    subordinates   subordinates

    ├───┤

83 Extrovert and outgoing   Introverted and reserved

    ├───┤

84 Treats medical staff as equals   Tends to be deferential when
                                            dealing with medical staff

├─────────────────────────────────────┤

85 Strives to achieve the best   Is satisfied with an average result
    possible result

├─────────────────────────────────────┤

86 Have moved around a lot in their   Have tended to stay in one area
    career, e.g. different jobs in NHS   or type of job
    and outside

├─────────────────────────────────────┤

87 Happier managing people rather   Happier managing systems or
    than systems or strategies   strategies rather than people

├─────────────────────────────────────┤

88 Pushes him-/herself forward   Does not push him-/herself
                                            forward

├─────────────────────────────────────┤

THANK YOU FOR TAKING THE TIME TO COMPLETE THIS QUESTIONNAIRE

References

Agor, W. (1985) The logic of intuition: How top executives make important decisions, *Organisational Dynamics*, 5: 18.

Alban-Metcalfe, B. (1983) How relevant is leadership research to the study of management effectiveness? A discussion and a suggested framework for skills training, *Personnel Review*, 12(3): 3–8.

Argyris, C. and Schon, D. A. L. (1978) *Organisational Learning: A Theory in Action Perspective*. Reading, MA: Addison-Wesley.

Banks, C. and Murphy, K. (1985) Towards narrowing the research-practice gap in performance appraisal, *Personnel Psychology*, 38: 335–44.

Bannister, B. and Fransella, E. (1971) *Inquiring Man: The Theory of Personal Constructs*. Harmondsworth: Penguin.

Beck, J. (1980) Changing a manager's construction of reality, in J. Beck and C. Cox (eds) *Advances in Management Education*. New York: Wiley & Son.

Bennis, W. and Nanus, B. (1985) *Leaders: The Strategies for Taking Charge*. New York: Harper and Row.

Bevan, S. and Thompson, M. (1992) An overview of policy and practice, in *Performance Management in the UK: An Analysis of the Issues*. Exeter: Institute of Personnel Management.

Boam, R. and Sparrow, P. (eds) (1992) *Focusing on Human Resources: A Competency-Based Approach*. London: McGraw-Hill.

Bovaird, T., Gregory, D. and Martin, S. (1988) Performance measurement in urban economic development, *Public Money & Management*, 8(4): 17–22.

Boyatzis, R. E. (1982) *The Competent Manager: A Model for Effective Performance*. New York: Wiley.

Burgoyne, J. (1976) Managerial effectiveness revisited, discussion paper. University of Lancaster.

Burgoyne, J. G. and Stewart, R. (1976) The nature, use and acquisition of managerial skills and other attributes, *Personnel Review*, 5(4): 19–29.

Campbell, S., Dunnett, M., Lawler, E. and Weick, K. (1970) *Managerial Behaviour Performance and Effectiveness*. London: McGraw-Hill.

Carter, N. (1989) Performance indicators: 'backseat driving' or 'hands-off control', *Policy and Politics*, 17(2): 131–8.

Dahrendorf, R. (1968) Homo sociologicus, in *Essays in the Theory of Society*. London: Routledge and Kegan Paul.

Day, P. and Klein, R. (1987) *Accountabilities: Five Public Services*. London: Tavistock.

Department of Health and Social Security (1986) *Individual Performance Review in the NHS*, official circular, Personnel Memorandum (86)10. London: HMSO.

Drucker, P. (1954) *The Practice of Management*. New York: Harper and Brothers.

Drucker, P. (1967) *The Effective Executive*. London: Heinemann.

Drucker, P. (1974) *Management Tasks, Responsibilities and Practices*. London: Harper and Row.

Drucker, P. (1990) *Managing the Non-profit Organisation*. Oxford: Butterworth Heinemann.

Drucker, P. (1992) *Managing for the Future*. Oxford: Butterworth Heinemann.

Dunn, N., Paulak, T. and Roberts, G. (1987) Cognitive performance appraisal: Mapping managers' category structure using the grid technique, *Personnel Review*, 16(3): 16–19.

Dunsire, A., Hartley, K. and Parker, D. (1994) Organisational status and performance: Summary of the findings, in D. J. McKevitt, and A. Lawaton (eds) *Public Sector Management: Theory, Critique and Practice*. London: Sage Publications.

Easterby-Smith, M. (1980) How to use repertory grids in human resource development, *Journal of European Industrial Training*, 4(2).

Feldman, J. (1981) Beyond attribution theory: Cognitive processes in performance appraisal, *Journal of Applied Psychology*, 66(2): 127–48.

Flanagan, H. (1990) A study of managerial effectiveness with particular reference to general managers in the NHS, MSocSc (Mode II: Research) thesis. University of Birmingham.

Flanagan, H. and Henry, P. (1993) *Healthy Working and Performance Management: A Survey of NHS organisations*. London: PBS.

Flanagan, H. and Thompson, D. (1993) Leadership: The swing of the pendulum, *Leadership and Organisation Development Journal*, 14(1): 9–15.

Fletcher, C. and Williams, R. (1992) Organisational experience, in *Performance Management in the UK: An Analysis of the Issues*. Exeter: Institute of Personnel Management.

Flynn, N. (1990) *Public Sector Management*. Hemel Hempstead: Harvester Wheatsheaf.

Fonda, N. and Stewart, R. (1994) Enactment in managerial jobs: A role analysis, *Journal of Management Studies*, 31(1): 83–103.

Garratt, R. (1991) *Learning to Lead*. Glasgow: Fontana.

Glaze, T. (1989) Cadbury's dictionary of competence, *Personnel Management*, July: 44–8.

Goldsmith, W. and Clutterbuck, D. (1984) *The Winning Streak*. London: Weidenfeld and Nicolson.

Gowler, D. and Legge, K. (1983) The meaning of management and the management of meaning: A view from social anthropology, in M. Earl (ed.) *Perspectives on Management: A Multi-Disciplinary Analysis*. Oxford: Oxford University Press.

Hales, C. P. (1986) What do managers do? A critical review of the evidence, *Journal of Management Studies*, 23(1): 88–115.

Hales, C. P. (1987) The manager's work in context: A pilot investigation of the relationship between management role demands and role performance, *Personnel Review*, 16(5): 26–33.

Handy, C. (1989) *The Age of Unreason*. London: Business Books.

Hannabuss, S. (1987) Collaborating over meanings in management, Drucker looks at effectiveness, *Personnel Review*, 16(5): 34–9.

Harrow, J. and Willcocks, L. (1990) Public services management: Activities, initiatives and limits to hearing, *Journal of Management Studies*, 27(3): 281–304.

Harvey-Jones, J. (1988) *Making it Happen*. London: Collins.

Harvey-Jones, J. (1992) *Troubleshooter 2*. London: BBC Books.

Helmreich, R. and Spencer, J. (1978) Competitiveness, *International Management*, 33(10): 23–4.

Herriot, P. (1989a) Selection as a social process, in M. Smith and I. T. Robertson (eds) *Advances in Selection and Assessment*. London: Wiley.

Herriot, P. (ed.) (1989b) *Assessment and Selection in Organisations*. New York: Wiley.

Hirsch, W. and Bevan, S. (1988) *What Makes a Manager? In Search of a Language for Management Skills*. University of Sussex: Institute of Manpower Studies.

Holmes, L. and Joyce, P. (1993) Rescuing the useful concept of managerial competence: From outcomes back to process, *Personnel Review*, 22(6): 37–52.

Howard, J. (1978) Ambition and the manager, *Management Today*, March: 82–6.

Iles, P. (1993) Achieving strategic coherence in HRD through competence-based management and organisation development, *Personnel Review*, 22(6): 63–80.

Institute of Personnel Management (1992) *Performance Management in the UK: An Analysis of the Issues*. Exeter: Institute of Personnel Management.

Isaac-Henry, K. and Painter, C. (1991) The management challenge in local government: Emerging trends, *Local Government Studies*, 17(3): 1169–89.

Isaac-Henry, K., Painter, C. and Barnes, C. (1993) *Management in the Public Sector: Challenge and Change*. London: Chapman and Hall.

Jackson, L. (1989) Turning airport managers into high fliers, *Personnel Management*, October: 80–5.

Janis, I. L. (1973) *Victims of Groupthink: A Psychological Study of Foreign Policy Decisions and Fiascos*. Boston, MA: Houghton Mifflin.

Johnson, G. K. (1992) Appraisal systems for continuous assessment and improvement of performance, *Recruitment, Selection and Retention*, 1(1): 11–15.

Jurgenson, C. E. (1966) Report to participants on an adjective word sort. Minneapolis Gas Company, Unpublished report, cited in S. Campbell, M. Dunnett, E. Lawler and K. Weick (eds) *Managerial Behaviour Performance and Effectiveness*. London: McGraw-Hill.

Kanter, R. (1984) *The Change Masters*. London: Allen and Unwin.

Katz, R. (1974) The skills of an effective administrator, *Harvard Business Review*, Sept/Oct: 90–103.

Kellner, P. and Crowther-Hunt, Lord (1980) *The Civil Servants: An Enquiry into Britain's Ruling Class*. London: Macdonald Futura.

Kelly, G. A. (1955) *The Psychology of Personal Constructs*, vols 1 and 2. New York: Norton.

Kirchoff, B. A. (1977) Organisation effectiveness measurement and policy research, *Academy of Management Review*, 2(3): 347–55.

Klein, R. (1982) Performance evaluation and the NHS: A case study in conceptual perplexity and organisational complexity, *Public Administration*, 60: 385–407.

Kolb, D., Lublin, S., Spoth, J. and Baker, R. (1986) Strategic management development: Experiential learning and managerial competencies, *Journal of Management Development*, 3(5): 18–24.

Kotter, J. (1982) *The General Managers.* New York: Macmillan.

Kotter, J. and Heskett, L. (1992) *Corporate Culture and Performance.* New York: Free Press.

Langford, V. (1979) Managerial effectiveness: A review of the literature, in M. Brodie and R. Bennett (eds) *Managerial Effectiveness.* Slough: Thames Valley Regional Management Centre.

Levenson, D. (1966) Role, personality and social structure, in L. Caser and B. Rosenburg (eds) *Sociological Theory: A Book of Readings.* New York: Macmillan.

Lewis, R. and Stewart, R. (1961) *The Boss: The Life and Times of the British Businessman.* London: Dent.

Lock, E., Mento, A. and Katchner, B. (1978) The interactions of ability and motivation in performance: an explanation of the many moderators, *Personnel Psychology*, 31(2): 269–80.

Lombardo, M. and McCall, M. (1982) Leaders on the line: Observations from a simulation of management work, in J. Hunt *et al.* (eds) *Leadership Beyond Establishment Views.* Carbondale: University of Illinois Press.

Machin, J. (1981) The expectations approach: A product of manager-led research which helps managers to improve their own effectiveness, in J. Machin, R. Stewart and C. Hales (eds) *Toward Management Effectiveness: Applied Research Perspectives on the Managerial Task.* Farnborough: Gower.

Machin, J. and Stewart, R. (1981) Directions for future research into managerial effectiveness, in J. Machin, R. Stewart and C. Hales (eds) *Toward Managerial Effectiveness: Applied Research Perspectives on the Management Task.* Farnborough: Gower.

Mann, S. and Pedler, M. (eds) (1992) *Biography in Management and Organisational Development.* Special issue of *Management Education and Development*, Autumn.

Marsh, D. (1991) Privatisation under Mrs Thatcher: A review of the literature, *Public Administration*, 69(4): 459–80.

McGregor, D. (1957) An uneasy look at performance appraisal, *Harvard Business Review*, 35(3): 89–94.

McGregor, D. (1960) *The Human Side of Enterprise.* London: McGraw-Hill.

McLelland, D. (1962) *The Achieving Society.* Princeton, NJ: Van Nostrand.

Meek, V. L. (1988) Organisational culture: Origins and weaknesses, *Organisation Studies*, 9(4): 453–73.

Miles, R. and Snow, C. (1978) *Organisational Strategy, Structure and Process.* Reading: McGraw-Hill.

Mintzberg, H. (1973) *The Nature of Managerial Work.* London: Harper and Row.

Mintzberg, H. (1983) *Power in and Around Organisations.* Englewood Cliffs, NJ: Prentice Hall.

Morgan, G. (1988) *Riding the Waves of Change: Developing Managerial Competencies for a Turbulent World.* San Francisco: Jossey-Bass.

Morse, J. and Wagner, F. (1978) Measuring the process of managerial effectiveness, *Academy of Management Journal*, 21(1): 23–35.

Moss Kanter, R. and Summers, D. V. (1987) Doing well while doing good: Dilemmas of performance measurement in non-profit organisations and the need for a multiple constituency approach, in W. W. Powell (ed.) *The Non-Profit Sector: A Research Handbook.* New Haven, CT: Yale University Press.

Nash, A. (1965) Vocational interests of effective managers: A review of the literature, *Personnel Psychology*, 18: 21–37.

Ouchi, W. (1981) *Theory 'Z': How American Business Should Meet the Japanese Challenge*. New York: Addison Wesley.

Pedler, M., Burgoyne, J. and Boydell, T. (1991) *The Learning Company: A Strategy for Sustainable Development*. Maidenhead: McGraw-Hill.

Peters, T. (1988) *Thriving on Chaos*. London: Macmillan.

Peters, T. (1992) *Liberation Management: Necessary Disorganisation for the Nanosecond Nineties*. London: Macmillan.

Peters, T. and Waterman, R. (1982) *In Search of Excellence*. London: Macmillan.

Pollitt, C. (1993) *Managerialism and the Public Services*, 2nd edn. Oxford: Blackwell.

Porter, L. and Lawler, E. (1968) *Managerial Attitudes and Performance*. Chicago, IL: Irwin-Dorsey.

Pye, A. (1988) Management competence in the public sector, *Public Money and Management*, Winter: 62–4.

Rackham, N. and Morgan, T. (1977) *Behaviour Analysis in Training*. London: McGraw Hill.

Reddin, W. J. (1970) *Management Effectiveness*. New York: McGraw-Hill.

Revans, R. W. (1982) The enterprise as a learning system, in R. W. Revans (ed.) *The Origins and Growth of Action Learning*. Bromley: Chartwell Bratt.

Sayles, L. B. (1979) *Leadership: What Effective Managers Really Do; and How They Do It*. New York: McGraw-Hill.

Schein, E. (1985) *Organisational Culture and Leadership*. San Francisco: Jossey-Bass.

Schroeder, H. M. (1989) *Managerial Competence: The Key to Excellence*. Iowa: Kendall Hunt.

Senge, P. M. (1992) *The Fifth Discipline: The Art and Practice of the Learning Organisation*. London: Century Business Press.

Sikorski, D. (1993) A general critique of the theory of public enterprise: Part II. How is public enterprise different from private? *International Journal of Public Sector Management*, 6(5): 56–67.

Sisson, K. and Storey, J. (1988) Developing effective managers: A review of the issue and an agenda for research, *Personnel Review*, 17(4): 3–8.

Skinner, B. F. (1953) *Science and Human Behavior*. New York: Macmillan.

Stamp, G. (1986) Management Styles, *Leadership and Organisation Development Journal*, 7(3): 27–33.

Stewart, A. and Stewart, V. (1981a) *Tomorrow's Managers Today*, 2nd edn. London: Institute of Personnel Management.

Stewart, A. and Stewart, V. (1981b) *Business Applications of Repertory Grid*. London: McGraw-Hill.

Stewart, J. (1980) *Understanding the Management of Local Government*. London: Longman.

Stewart, J. and Walsh, K. (1992) Change in the management of public service, *Public Administration*, 70(4): 499–518.

Stewart, R. (1967) *Managers and Their Jobs*. Maidenhead: McGraw-Hill.

Stewart, R. (1976) *Contrasts in Management*. Maidenhead: McGraw-Hill.

Stewart, R. (1989a) *Leading in the NHS: A Practical Guide*. Basingstoke: Macmillan.

Stewart, R. (1989b) Studies of managerial jobs and behaviour: The ways forward, *Journal of Management Studies*, 26(1): 1–10.

Stewart, R., Smith, P., Blake, J. and Wingate, P. (1980) *The District Administration in the NHS*, London: Pitman.

Thompson, D., Harrison, J. and Flanagan, H. (1994) Managing people: The breakfast menu, *Health Manpower Review*, 20(1): 30–5.

Tsui, A. S. (1984) A multiple constituency framework of reputational effectiveness, in J. Hunt *et al.* (eds) *Leaders and Managers: International Perspectives on Managerial Behaviour and Leadership*. New York: Pergamon.

Wickett, P. R. and McFarland, B. (1967) *Measuring Executive Effectiveness*. Appleton Century Croft.

Willcocks, S. G. (1992) Managerial effectiveness and the public sector: A health service example, *International Journal of Public Sector Management*, 5(5): 4–10.

Williams, A., Dobson, P. and Walters, M. (1993) *Changing Culture: New Organisational Approaches*, 2nd edn. London: Institute of Personnel Management.

Williams, D. (1985) *Better Management, Better Health*. Bristol: NHS Training Authority.

Index

DELIVERING WELFARE
THE GOVERNANCE OF THE SOCIAL SERVICES IN THE 1990s

Tony Butcher

Recent years have seen a series of radical changes in the arrangements for the delivery of education, housing, health and other major social services. Local authorities are being transformed from front line delivery agencies of the welfare state into enabling authorities. Privatization, marketization and the search for efficiency are now important features of the system of welfare delivery. The Citizen's Charter and other developments reflect a growing concern with consumerism and customer sensitivity.

This book provides an up-to-date survey of the role of central government, local authorities, the health services and other agencies responsible for delivering the social services, and the directions that welfare delivery has taken in recent years. At a time when the organization of welfare delivery and the quality of the public services are high on the political agenda, it provides a timely study of an important subject. It will be of interest to both students and practitioners in social policy, public administration and politics.

Contents
Introduction – Part I: The public face of welfare – Central government and welfare – The government of welfare outside Whitehall – The coordination and planning of welfare – Accountability and the public – Part II: New directions in the delivery of welfare – The rolling back of the local welfare state – The privatization of welfare delivery – The search for efficiency and value for money – The customer orientation – Conclusion – Further reading – References – Index.

208pp   0 335 15710 6 (Paperback)   0 335 15711 4 (Hardback)

MANAGING

Graeme Salaman

There has never been more urgent need to identify and develop the skills of effective management. Current programmes of organizational change in public and private sector organizations place enormous burden on, while simultaneously transforming, the nature and functions of the manager. There has been a great deal of work on identifying the skills or competences of managers but these efforts have limited value.

Graeme Salaman offers a new and more radical conception of managerial work, and what is required for managers to develop the requisite skills. He offers a conceptual model of management – as responsibility for the quality of subordinates' work – and identifies the constituent skills necessary for the effective management of others' performance. His view of management is based on management learning, and he offers models of how people learn, and how to help others learn. He also suggests that for most managers, the key skills of management are not only difficult, they are actually counter to their normal working habits. They have frequently been trained to be incompetent. He provides practical suggestions for overcoming their resistances and for developing the appropriate management skills.

Contents

Introduction – The role of management skills in today's organizations – What do managers do? – What are the key management skills? – The management role – The management of performance and learning – Achieving learning – Barriers to learning – The learning organization – The importance of management style – Improving the management of learning – References – Index.

160pp   0 335 19363 3 (paperback)   0 335 19364 1 (hardback)

CONTROLLING HEALTH PROFESSIONALS
THE FUTURE OF WORK AND ORGANIZATION IN THE NHS

Stephen Harrison and Christopher Pollitt

For twenty years, British governments of both the left and right have tried to improve the management of the NHS. But the distinctive contribution of the Thatcher governments of the 1980s has defined this very much in terms of controlling health professionals: doctors, nurses and others. This volume

- offers an explanation of why this approach was adopted
- examines in detail the various methods of control employed
- assesses the consequences for the future of professional work and organization in the NHS.

The book will be of interest to a wide range of health professionals, including nurses, doctors, health authority members and managers and will also be useful for students of social policy and health studies.

Contents
Professionals and managers – Finance for health care: supply, demand and rationing – Challenging the professionals – Incorporating the professionals – Changing the environment – The future of managerial and professional work in the NHS – Notes – References – Index.

192pp   0 335 09643 3 (Paperback)   0 335 09644 1 (Hardback)